WHO PAYS FOR DEVELOPMENT?

HOUSING, MONEY

&

POWER IN AMERICAN CITIES

B. LIBRE KAFELE

LIBREWORLD
PRESS

WHO PAYS FOR DEVELOPMENT?

HOUSING, MONEY

&

POWER IN AMERICAN CITIES

B. LIBRE KAFELE

LIBREWORLD PRESS

This book is dedicated to:

The cities that were never allowed to fail or to prosper, shaped instead by administrative design, capital allocation, or monetary power.

The communities that absorbed debt, poverty, and deprivation while capital fled elsewhere.

The planners, policymakers, builders, and urban residents who understand that urban outcomes are products of institutional design.

Those who recognize that cities are not symbols, but systems where land, capital, and people intersect and respond to pressure.

And my family, friends, loved ones, and ancestors who have lived in cities, or migrated to them, in search of better opportunities.

Acknowledgments

This book emerged from readings, lived experiences, observations, and interactions from an interdisciplinary study of urban planning, urban studies, monetary economics, finance, and political economy.

I express my gratitude to the practitioners, scholars, and policymakers whose work helped clarify and corroborate how cities function as financial and social systems. These insights emerged from the author's observation of how capital, policy, land, and real assets interact under administrative and institutional constraints. These insights were shaped by careful observation of how capital, policy, land, and real assets interact within administrative and institutional constraints.

I also acknowledge the cities and their comparative patterns across regions and regime — evidence that urban outcomes are structured, shaped, and directed by institutional design.

Other works by B. LIBRE KAFELE include

"CAPITAL IN THE CITY: *URBAN DEVELOPMENT, SOCIO-ECONOMIC INFLATION*

&

MONETARY POWER"

Table of Contents

Preface:

Why This Book Exists

This book was written because urban development is routinely discussed without honesty about cost.

Residents are told development is inevitable. Policymakers are told it is necessary. Investors are told it is efficient. Housing agencies are told it is constrained by forces beyond their control.

Each of these claims contains some truth. Taken together, however, they obscure the most important question cities consistently avoid: who pays when development happens, Who pays when it fails? And who benefits when it succeeds?

Urban development is not simply a matter of buildings or zoning. It is a financial system that distributes risk, protection, and reward unevenly across neighborhoods and populations, often along spatial and racial lines. These distributions are shaped by monetary policy, municipal finance, and institutional incentives that are rarely explained in plain language to those most affected by them.

This book does not argue against development. It argues against unexamined development: development that privatizes upside while socializing risk, treats displacement as unfortunate but unavoidable, and mistakes financial engineering for progress.

The goal is clarity, not persuasion. The arguments that follow are not ideological; they are structural. They trace how money moves through cities, how decisions made far from neighborhoods shape life on the block, and why distrust of development is often a rational response to repeated exposure to loss.

This book is written for multiple audiences: residents trying to understand why their neighborhoods keep changing; policymakers and housing agencies navigating institutional constraints; and investors seeking returns without destabilizing the communities that make those returns possible.

If cities are serious about economic, social and fiscal sustainability, they must begin with honesty. And honesty begins with a question too often avoided:

Who is paying—and for whose benefit?

Part I: SEEING THE SYSTEM

CHAPTER 1: A Block, a Budget, a Balance Sheet

On one block, houses stand boarded up and vacant. Windows are sealed with plywood, paint peels from brick façades, and trash gathers where front steps once led to occupied homes. A few streets away, new construction rises behind banners announcing *Revitalization Is Here*. Renderings promise walkability, safety, and opportunity.

Both blocks exist in the same city.

Both appear in the same municipal budget.

Yet only one is treated as an investment.

Urban development is rarely discussed in these terms. More often, it is framed as a matter of design, zoning, or community preference. Public debate centers on building height, architectural style, or density limits. Residents are invited to participate in hearings where the scope of discussion is carefully managed: aesthetic concerns are welcomed, while questions about financing, risk, and long-term cost are treated as technical or premature.

This framing obscures the central reality of urban change. Cities do not transform primarily because of design decisions. They transform because of financial decisions about borrowing, access to credit, guarantees, and the allocation of risk among public institutions, private capital, and residents.

To understand development, one must look beyond the block to the budget—and beyond the budget to the balance sheet.

One Neighborhood, Multiple Narratives

Cities routinely describe the same neighborhood in different ways, depending on the audience. To residents, an area may be labeled *"distressed," "underutilized,"* or *"in need of revitalization."* To investors, it becomes *"emerging," "undervalued,"* or *"well-positioned for growth."* To federal agencies, it is reclassified as a *"qualified census tract," "target area,"* or *"opportunity zone."*

These descriptions are not merely rhetorical. They are financial narratives that justify intervention, unlock funding streams, and shape expectations about risk and return. As scholars of urban political economy have long argued, cities are not neutral spaces but arenas in which competing actors struggle to define land, value, and responsibility.[1]

What separates a *"declining"* neighborhood from an *"emerging"* one is often not the condition of the housing stock or the needs of residents, but the availability of capital and the willingness of institutions to underwrite risk. As Cedric Robinson theorizes in his book entitled, *"On Racial Capitalism, Black Internationalism, and Cultures of Resistance"*, these disparities are not incidental; they are produced by a system in which capital accumulation is inseparable from racial hierarchies, resulting in structurally unequal access to investment and protection.[2]

---

[1] Michael C. Lens, *"Zoning, Land Use, and the Reproduction of Urban Inequality,"* Annual Review of Sociology 48, no. 1 (July 2022): 421–39, https://doi.org/10.1146/annurev-soc-030420-122027

[2] Cedric J. Robinson, "Oliver Cromwell Cox and the Historiography of the West," in On Racial Capitalism, Black Internationalism, and Cultures of Resistance (London: Pluto Press, 2019), 79.

A Block, a Budget, a Balance Sheet

Municipal and financial infrastructures operate within incentive-based systems that are deeply interconnected with federal and global economies. Historical racial hierarchies—codified through redlining, state-sponsored segregation, and global financial extraction—have institutionalized inequality. Their effects remain visible in the social conditions and economic outcomes of cities and neighborhoods, often along lines of race and class. Two blocks—even two cities—with similar physical characteristics can experience radically different futures because one is surrounded by financing mechanisms that absorb uncertainty, while the other remains exposed.

The way a neighborhood is described publicly is not only rhetorical, it reflects the financial and policy mechanisms that shape development. Understanding these mechanisms requires examining municipal budgets and fiscal decision-making. Jersey City's Pacific Avenue corridor illustrates these dynamics locally, but similar processes occur across U.S. cities. Targeted fiscal incentives can facilitate capital flow while shifting risk onto long-term residents.

Development as a Fiscal Decision

Local governments are often portrayed as reactive responding to market forces rather than shaping them. In this view, private capital leads and the public sector follow. This narrative understates the extent to which urban development is the product of deliberate fiscal choice.

Municipal governments decide:

- whether to issue debt, and at what cost;
- whether to grant tax abatements or exemptions;

- whether to guarantee loans or provide credit enhancements; and
- whether to invest public resources in infrastructure that increases land values.

These decisions determine which projects are viable and which never move beyond the proposal stage.[3] Development "feasibility" is not a neutral assessment; it is the outcome of policy choices embedded in financial systems.

Urban sociologists and political economists have described this dynamic as the operation of a *"growth machine"* in which public officials, developers, financiers, and property owners align around increasing land values.[4,5] Growth, in this context, is not simply about meeting housing need or accommodating population change. It is about structuring opportunities for accumulation within a given fiscal and political framework. Scholars such as John R. Logan and Harvey Molotch describe cities as arenas in which land-use interests compete for public money and attempt to shape decisions that determine land-use outcomes. Each locality, in striving to make these gains, is in competition with other localities because the degree of growth, at least at any given

---

[3] Rachel Weber, *"Embedding Futurity in Urban Governance: Redevelopment Schemes and the Time Value of Money,"* Environment and Planning A: Economy and Space 53, no. 3 (2021): 503–24, https://doi.org/10.1177/0308518X20936686

[4] Barbara Ferman, *Challenging the Growth Machine: Neighborhood Politics in Chicago and Pittsburgh* (Lawrence: University Press of Kansas, 1996).

[5] Harvey Molotch, "The City as a Growth Machine: Toward a Political Economy of Place," American Journal of Sociology 82, no. 2 (1976): 309–32, http://www.jstor.org/stable/2777096

moment, is finite. The scarcity of developmental resources means that government becomes the arena in which land-use interest groups compete for public money and attempt to mold those decisions which will determine the land-use outcomes. Localities thus compete with one another to gain the *preconditions* of growth."[6]

This does not imply that development is inherently predatory, or that public officials act in bad faith. It does mean that incentives matter and that those incentives shape which neighborhoods are stabilized, which are transformed, and which are left to absorb decline.

What Budgets Show and What They Hide

Municipal budgets are often treated as technical documents, accessible primarily to specialists. In reality, they are political texts—revealing priorities while obscuring mechanisms.

A capital improvement plan may allocate substantial funds to infrastructure in redevelopment districts while devoting comparatively little to maintenance in long-established residential areas. Housing budgets may emphasize the number of units produced without addressing long-term affordability, neighborhood-level displacement, or fiscal exposure.

Most significantly, budgets rarely make visible the contingent liabilities associated with development— loan guarantees, tax abatements, and foregone revenues that

---

[6] Molotch, "City as a Growth Machine," 312.

represent real public costs, even when they do not appear as immediate expenditures.[7]

Municipal fiscal tools—including PILOT agreements, tax abatements, redevelopment incentives, and Opportunity Zone designations—illustrate how cities actively structure investment and risk in urban neighborhoods. These mechanisms are often described as ways to "encourage development" or "stimulate private investment." In practice, they reduce developer exposure—through lowered or deferred taxes, credit enhancements, or special zoning allowances—while channeling public resources and benefits into targeted areas.

Such incentives do not simply facilitate construction; they shape which neighborhoods attract capital, which projects become viable, and which residents bear the costs. For example, a PILOT agreement reduces property tax obligations for developers in exchange for new construction, effectively subsidizing investment in a specific tract. Similarly, Opportunity Zones provide federal tax benefits for investors who purchase property in designated areas, concentrating capital in neighborhoods historically excluded from equitable investment. Redevelopment incentives and tax abatements work in tandem, creating a fiscal landscape in which the city actively directs capital flows, elevates property values, and reshapes social and economic conditions—even while long-term residents absorb rising costs and displacement pressures. While such mechanisms can facilitate development that might not otherwise occur,

---

[7] Polackova, Hana. "Contingent Government Liabilities: A Hidden Fiscal Risk." Finance & Development 36, no. 1 (March 1999). https://www.imf.org/external/pubs/ft/fandd/1999/03/polackov.htm

they also redistribute fiscal resources in ways that are often opaque to residents and difficult to evaluate over time.[8]

Municipal budgets often reveal a patterned prioritization of capital expenditures toward infrastructure in redevelopment districts—often the same areas as or adjacent to federally designated Opportunity Zones —while devoting comparatively little to maintenance in long-established residential areas (see historical redlining patterns and opportunity zone maps).[9] Comparatively, investments and tax breaks offered "in the name of revitalization" in historically redlined neighborhoods—areas once designated as "undesirable" or "at risk" by the Home Owners' Loan Corporation (HOLC) and the Federal Housing Administration prior to the Fair Housing Act of 1968—can contribute to processes now described as gentrification.[10] The term "gentrification" was coined by the British sociologist Ruth Glass to describe the socio-economic transformation in London neighborhoods in the 1960s.[11] Glass used the term to describe the transformation of

---

[8] David B. Lawrence and Susan C. Stephenson, "The Economics and Politics of Tax Increment Financing," *Growth and Change* 26, no. 1 (1995): 105–37, https://doi.org/10.1111/j.1468-2257.1995.tb00163.x

[9] Digital Scholarship Lab, University of Richmond, "Mapping Inequality: Redlining in New Deal America," accessed February 21, 2026, https://dsl.richmond.edu/panorama/redlining/map#loc=4/40.4939/-95.8425

[10] U.S. Department of Housing and Urban Development, *Opportunity Zones* dataset, HUD User GIS Open Data, accessed February 21, 2026, https://hudgis-hud.opendata.arcgis.com/datasets/HUD::opportunity-zones/explore?location=28.420892%2C0.315564%2C0

[11] D. Schlossberg, *"What Do We Talk About When We Talk About Gentrification?"* Journal of Affordable Housing & Community Development Law 25, no. 2 (2017): 215–218, https://www.jstor.org/stable/26408186

working-class neighborhoods through middle- and upper-class in-migration, resulting in displacement and a shift in social character.[12] This term has since been widely adopted across urban sociology, economics, policy, and planning to describe the financialized transformation of urban space.

Etymologically, "gentrification" derives from "gentry," meaning nobility of rank or birth, with origins in the fourteenth century and roots in the Old French *genterie*.[13] The term catalyzed to utilization and popularization within the lexicon of American sociologists, economists, urban planners, policy makers, activists and real estate agents and developers alike to describe an urban phenomenon where residents of a higher socio-economic status migrate into a neighborhood or community causing demographic shifts and inflation in property values causing changes to the demography, economy, land scape and "desirability" of the neighborhood, community or city over time.[14]

This uneven fiscal geography reflects what Molotch describes as the structural power of the urban growth coalition, in which public spending decisions are oriented toward land value intensification rather than neighborhood stability. Historical redlining practices documented by Rothstein and Taylor further show how contemporary budgetary disparities are layered onto earlier regimes of racially differentiated credit access, while Desmond's work shows how these dynamics materialize as housing precarity

---

[12] Schlossberg, *"What Do We Talk About When We Talk About Gentrification?"* 215-218

[13] Merriam-Webster, s.v. "gentry," accessed February 21, 2026, https://www.merriam-webster.com/dictionary/gentry

[14] Schlossberg, *"What Do We Talk About When We Talk About Gentrification?"* 215-218

at the household level.[15][16][17] The result is a budgeting process that prioritizes growth while minimizing public discussion of risk of displacement, inflation and social instability for the residents. For example, in the author's hometown of Jersey City and surrounding municipalities in Hudson County, a circa-1940 redlining map from the Mapping Inequality shows the downtown district graded as "hazardous" (red) and "undesirable" (yellow). The area's population was primarily Italian, Irish, and Polish, with a growing Black population estimated at roughly 30 percent.[18]

Within the Pacific Avenue residential area—comprising Pacific Avenue, Woodward, Van Horne, Whiton, and Halladay Streets—occupancy rates were roughly 90 percent, of which approximately 30 percent represented owner-occupied housing. Area descriptions at the time reported virtually no sales demand. Property values ranged between $2,000 and $3,500. When adjusted for inflation from 1939 to 2025, these figures are equivalent to roughly $46,636 to $81,600 in 2025 dollars, representing an increase of more

---

[15] Matthew Desmond, Evicted: Poverty and Profit in the American City (New York: Crown Publishers, 2016).

[16] Richard Rothstein, *The Color of Law: A Forgotten History of How Our Government Segregated America* (New York: Liveright Publishing, 2017).

[17] Keeanga-Yamahtta Taylor, Race for Profit: How Banks and the Real Estate Industry Undermined Black Homeownership (Chapel Hill: University of North Carolina Press, 2019).

[18] Digital Scholarship Lab, University of Richmond, *Mapping Inequality: Redlining in New Deal America*, accessed February 21, 2026, "D27—Hudson County, New Jersey," https://dsl.richmond.edu/panorama/redlining/map/NJ/HudsonCo/area_descriptions/D27#mapview=full&loc=15/40.7097/-74.0526

than twenty-threefold over the period.[19] The rent bracket for the area was \$12.50-\$15.00 which is equivalent to \$279.82 to \$349.77 in purchasing power.[20]

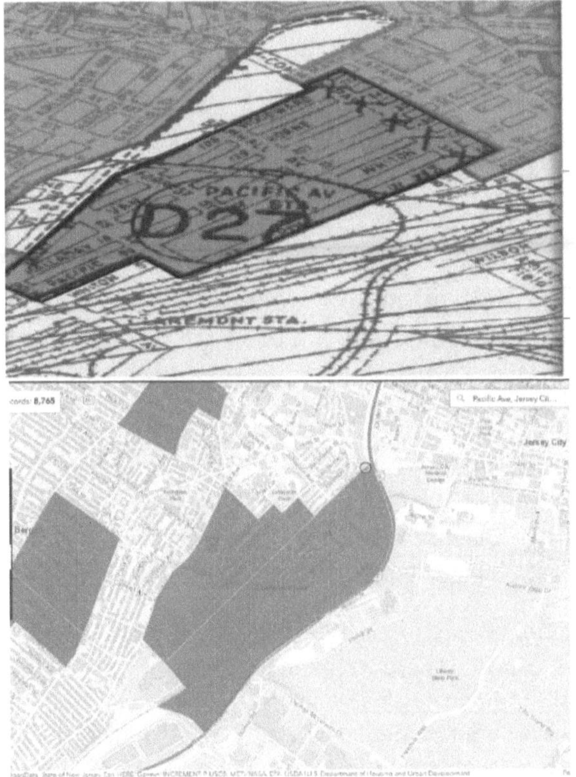

Figure 1.1: Historical Redlining and Contemporary Opportunity in the Pacific/Communipaw Ave Neighborhood in Downtown Jersey City

Side-by-side comparison shows substantial spatial overlap between areas graded "Hazardous" by the Home Owners'

---

[19] Digital Scholarship Lab, *Mapping Inequality*, "D27—Hudson County, New Jersey."

[20] Digital Scholarship Lab, *Mapping Inequality*, "D27⬚—⬚Hudson County, New Jersey."

Loan Corporation in the 1930s and census tracts later designated as Opportunity Zones. The shift reflects not a neutral rediscovery of distressed space, but a revaluation of previously marginalized urban land under new financial logics.[21]

Contemporary data from the U.S. Census Bureau indicate that median home values in the census tracts encompassing the Pacific Avenue corridor now exceed $571,700, while median gross rents have risen to approximately $2,129 per month.[22][23] Median gross rents are approximated using ACS Table B25104: Monthly Housing Costs (U.S. Census Bureau, 2020–2024 ACS 5-Year Estimates). This includes utilities and, for owners, mortgage payments and taxes.[24]

---

[21] U.S. Department of Housing and Urban Development, "Opportunity Zones," ArcGIS Open Data, accessed February 22, 2026, https://hudgis-hud.opendata.arcgis.com/datasets/HUD::opportunity-zones/explore
; and Mapping Inequality, Digital Scholarship Lab, University of Richmond, accessed February 22, 2026, https://dsl.richmond.edu/panorama/redlining/map

[22] U.S. Census Bureau, "Median Value (Dollars)," American Community Survey, ACS 1-Year Estimates Detailed Tables, Table B25077, accessed on February 19, 2026, https://data.census.gov/table/ACSDT1Y2024.B25077?g=040XX00US34,34_050XX00US34017,34017_060XX00US3401736000,3401736000_1400000US34017004600.

[23] U.S. Census Bureau. "Median Monthly Housing Costs (Dollars)." American Community Survey, ACS 5-Year Estimates Detailed Tables, Table B25105, https://data.census.gov/table/ACSDT5Y2024.B25105?g=040XX00US34,34_050XX00US34017,34017_060XX00US3401736000,3401736000_1400000US34017004600. Accessed on 19 Feb 2026.

[24] U.S. Census Bureau. "Median Monthly Housing Costs (Dollars)." American Community Survey, ACS 5-Year Estimates Detailed Tables, Table B25105,

The dramatic rise from an inflation-adjusted $46,636–$81,600 in 1940 to over $571,700 today illustrates a profound revaluation of capital in the Pacific Avenue corridor. This increase is not merely the product of natural market demand; rather, it reflects deliberate fiscal and policy choices that direct development toward neighborhoods historically denied equitable investment. Infrastructure improvements, and redevelopment incentives concentrate capital in targeted districts, amplifying property values while long-term residents face escalating costs. Today, this specific neighborhood in the Downtown district of Jersey City is located in an area designated as an "Opportunity Zone." Opportunity Zones are census tracts designated under the 2017 Tax Cuts and Jobs Act to attract private investment through preferential capital gains tax treatment.[25] Investors who place capital into Qualified Opportunity Funds can defer and reduce tax liability, creating a federally subsidized incentive to channel capital into areas officially classified as "distressed."[26] In practice, many of these tracts overlap significantly with neighborhoods historically marked as *hazardous* on Home Owners' Loan Corporation (HOLC) redlining maps (See Figure 1.1).[27] The spatial continuity is not incidental. Areas once excluded from mortgage credit are now selectively reintegrated into capital markets—but on

---

[25] Brett Theodos et al., *An Early Assessment of Opportunity Zones for Equitable Development Projects* (Washington, DC: Urban Institute, 2018), 1–10, https://www.urban.org/sites/default/files/publication/102348/early-assessment-of-opportunity-zones-for-equitable-development-projects.pdf

[26] Theodos et al., Early Assessment of Opportunity Zones, 1–10.

[27] Source: HUD Opportunity Zones dataset; *Mapping Inequality*, University of Richmond Digital Scholarship Lab.

terms structured around investor return rather than resident stability.

The policy does not simply target poverty; it re-financializes historically disinvested space. What was once redlined out of credit is now redlined into speculative capital flows. As the map illustrates, the Pacific Avenue neighborhood in Downtown Jersey City is located in and adjacent to one of the Opportunity Zones which plays a quintessential role in the gentrification of the neighborhood in conjunction with the City of Jersey City. Such patterns align closely with Molotch's analysis of the urban growth machine, in which municipal spending, developer influence, and land speculation converge to structure urban opportunity around capital accumulation rather than neighborhood stability.[28]

Historical credit discrimination further shaped these outcomes. As Rothstein and Taylor document, the HOLC and FHA effectively excluded Black and other marginalized residents from fair mortgage access, embedding structural inequities that persist today.[29] The subsequent influx of investment into previously "undesirable" tracts—through public subsidies, private capital, or mixed-use redevelopment henceforth produces a form of capital capture in which the benefits of rising property values disproportionately benefit new entrants and investors, while long-term residents bear the risks of displacement and financial precarity. Desmond's research underscores how these dynamics materialize at the household level, producing

---

[28] Molotch, "City as a Growth Machine," 312.
[29] Rothstein, The Color of Law, 60–63; Taylor, Race for Profit, 25–91.

eviction, housing instability, and constrained mobility, even as neighborhoods are celebrated as "revitalized."[30]

This process is simultaneously local and global. Aalbers highlights the financialization of housing as a mechanism that transforms urban space into an investment vehicle, while Wetzstein situates these trends within broader patterns of global housing affordability crises, showing that similar logics operate across major cities worldwide.[31] Robinson's framework of racial capitalism provides a structural lens to interpret these phenomena: the extraction of value from historically marginalized communities is not incidental but embedded in the political and financial systems that govern urban development.[32] Together, these perspectives suggest that the trajectory of Pacific Avenue is neither accidental nor inevitable; it is the material outcome of intersecting fiscal policy, capital flows, and racialized market logics.

A concrete illustration of these dynamics can be seen in the Paulus Hook redevelopment in downtown Jersey City.[33] The project was structured under a 30-year Payment In Lieu Of Taxes (PILOT) agreement, reducing the developer's property tax obligations in exchange for high-density,

---

[30] Desmond, *Evicted*.

[31] Steffen Wetzstein, "The Global Urban Housing Affordability Crisis," *Urban Studies* 54, no. 14 (2017): 3159–77, https://www.jstor.org/stable/26428376

[32] Robinson, "Oliver Cromwell Cox and the Historiography of the West," 79.

[33] Daniel Ulloa, "Jersey City Council Votes in Favor of 30-Year PILOT for Paulus Hook Development," *Hudson County View*, October 9, 2025, https://hudsoncountyview.com/jersey-city-council-votes-in-favor-of-30-year-pilot-for-paulus-hook-development/

mixed-use construction.[34] By temporarily lowering fiscal exposure for the developer, the PILOT facilitated capital investment in an area with a legacy of redlining.[35] The city, in turn, assumes short-term revenue loss and relies on projected increases in property values and economic activity to justify the agreement. This arrangement exemplifies how public funds, incentives, and municipal budgeting decisions channel capital into specific neighborhoods, producing rising property values and reshaping social composition, while long-term residents bear much of the financial and social risk. As Molotch observes in Urban Fortunes, these patterns reflect the structural power of the urban growth coalition, while Rothstein and Taylor demonstrate how historical inequities persist in contemporary credit and investment flows.[36]

These patterns are evident across the United States—from the Clinton Hill, Fort Greene, and Bedford-Stuyvesant neighborhoods of Brooklyn and Harlem in New York City to the Mission District of San Francisco, and even in Hoboken, a municipality adjacent to Jersey City. Historically, Hoboken contained substantial Black and Latino working-class populations; however, decades of disinvestment followed by rapid reinvestment and gentrification have transformed its demographic and economic profile. By 2023, the city was approximately 68% white, with a median property value of about $872,100

---

[34] Ulloa, "Jersey City Council Votes in Favor of 30-Year PILOT for Paulus Hook

[35] Digital Scholarship Lab, *Mapping Inequality: Redlining in New Deal America*, Hudson County, New Jersey (Downtown Jersey City near Paulus Hook Development), redlining map

[36] Molotch, "City as a Growth Machine," 310; Rothstein, *The Color of Law*, 60–63; Taylor, *Race for Profit*, 25–91.

according to U.S. Census–derived data. Notably, Home Owners' Loan Corporation (HOLC) maps from the late 1930s classified large portions of Hoboken as "hazardous" or "undesirable," illustrating the long-term spatial legacy of redlining.[373839] There are numerous examples across the United States in which extractive financial practices and speculative real estate investment have produced outcomes whereby costs are localized and borne by residents, while gains are privatized and concentrated among economic elites. Taken together, this historical and contemporary evidence demonstrates that urban development is not an inevitable process but one that is structured, financed, and governed in ways that determine who benefits, who bears risk, and who ultimately pays.

The Balance Sheet Behind Revitalization

Every development project rests on an implicit balance sheet. Assets include land, buildings, and projected revenue streams. Liabilities include debt service, operating costs, and exposure to market volatility. What distinguishes public-sector involvement in development is not the absence of risk, but the capacity to redistribute it.

When projects succeed, rising property values and rents are celebrated as evidence of market efficiency. When they

---

[37] U.S. Census Bureau, QuickFacts: *Hoboken city, New Jersey*, accessed February 21, 2026,
https://www.census.gov/quickfacts/fact/table/hobokencitynewjersey/PST045224
[38] Data USA, *Hoboken, NJ – Profile*, accessed February 21, 2026,
https://datausa.io/profile/geo/hoboken-nj?redirect=true
[39] Digital Scholarship Lab, *Mapping Inequality: Redlining in New Deal America*, Hudson County, New Jersey (Hoboken, New Jersey), redlining map

falter, municipalities absorb costs through refinancing, service reductions, deferred maintenance, or future tax increases. Residents experience these adjustments not as accounting entries, but as diminished services, higher housing costs, and increased instability.

This pattern helps explain persistent distrust of development in many urban communities. Residents are not opposing change itself; they are responding to a repeated experience in which they absorb downside risk without sharing proportionately in the upside.[40]

Under these conditions, revitalization serves less as a neutral program of improvement than as a risk-management regime that systematically displaces exposure from capital onto households with the least capacity to absorb loss.

Why the Block Remains Central

Focusing on the block is not rhetorical; it is analytical. Neighborhoods are where fiscal decisions materialize as lived experience. Borrowing costs translate into rent increases. Tax abatements granted to new developments produce budget constraints elsewhere, often in schools, maintenance, and social services. Infrastructure investments reshape property values unevenly, amplifying gains in some areas while accelerating pressures in other.

Research on urban inequality consistently shows that development reorganizes disparity rather than simply

---

[40] Mindy Thompson Fullilove, "Urban Renewal," in *Root Shock: How Tearing Up City Neighborhoods Hurts America, and What We Can Do About It*, 52–70 (New York: NYU Press, 2016), https://doi.org/10.2307/j.ctt21pxmmc.9

responding to it.[41] Growth does not eliminate inequality; it redistributes it spatially—concentrating stability and opportunity in some neighborhoods while exporting volatility and precarity to others.

Understanding this requires moving beyond moral debates about fairness or cultural arguments about neighborhood character. It requires examining the financial architecture of urban development—specifically how risk, reward, and responsibility are allocated across public institutions, private capital, and residents.

That examination begins by acknowledging a basic fact often obscured by market-rhetoric: development is not inevitable. It is structured, financed, and governed through policy choices that determine who is protected, who is exposed, and who ultimately pays.

Conclusion: Seeing Development Clearly

This chapter has argued that urban development cannot be understood solely at the level of buildings or blocks. It must be analyzed through municipal budgets and financial balance sheets that shape decision-making long before construction begins—often before residents are aware that change is underway.

When these structures are made visible, patterns emerge. Similar neighborhoods receive different treatment not because of intrinsic qualities, cultural characteristics or resident behavior, but because of how risk is priced,

---

[41] Rachael A. Woldoff, review of *Stuck in Place: Urban Neighborhoods and the End of Progress toward Racial Equality*, by Patrick Sharkey, American Journal of Sociology 121, no. 1 (2015): 288–90, https://doi.org/10.1086/681080

distributed, and absorbed across institutions. Skepticism toward development is therefore not ideological; it is experiential—grounded in repeated exposure to loss without commensurate protection or gain.

The chapters that follow extend this analysis outward, linking neighborhood change to monetary policy, institutional incentives, and national financial systems operating far beyond the scale of any single city. But the core insight remains:

Urban development is not just about what is built.

It is about who carries risk, who receives protection, and who pays when projections fail.

Until cities confront that reality directly—at the level of finance, governance, and accountability—debates about design, density, and revitalization will continue to miss the point.

Public Subsidy (PILOT)/Opportunity Zones/Tax Abatement/Redevelopment Initiative

↓

Reduced Developer Risk

↓

Capital Inflow / Redevelopment

↓

Rising Property Values

↓

Long-Term Resident Displacement / Financial Exposure

Figure 1.2: *This figure illustrates the typical causal pathway through which publicly supported redevelopment initiatives reshape neighborhood housing markets. Programs such as PILOT agreements, tax abatements, and redevelopment designations reduce upfront risk for private developers by stabilizing expected returns and lowering carrying costs. Once risk is compressed, capital flows more readily into the targeted area, accelerating new construction and property turnover. These investments contribute to rising property values and rent levels, which in turn increase cost burdens and financial exposure for incumbent residents. Over time, the cumulative effect is the displacement—direct or indirect—of long-term households, not as an unintended byproduct, but as a predictable outcome of a development model structured around risk-adjusted capital attraction.*

CHAPTER 2: Development Is a Financing Decision

Development rarely begins where people think it does.

It does not begin at a planning meeting or a zoning hearing. It does not begin with an architect's drawing or a community visioning session. By the time those moments occur, the most consequential decision has already been made often quietly, and often elsewhere.

The decision is whether a project can be financed.

Before a single unit is designed, a site is evaluated according to debt service requirements, projected cash flow, underwriting assumptions, and exposure to risk. Lenders and investors assess whether anticipated revenues can service debt, satisfy return thresholds, and withstand market volatility. If the numbers do not work, the project ends there. Need does not rescue it. Community support does not save it. Policy priorities do not override it. The project disappears, not because it was unwanted, but because it was deemed *unfundable*.

This is the first reality of urban development: it is not primarily a planning exercise. It is a credit judgment.

How Feasibility Becomes Fate

Cities often explain development outcomes by invoking feasibility. Projects that proceed are said to "pencil out."

Development Is a Financing Decision

Those that do not are dismissed as unrealistic. The language carries the authority of mathematics, suggesting neutrality, objectivity and inevitability.

But feasibility is not discovered. It is produced.

In practice, the appearance of viability is heavily shaped by policy instruments that restructure project economics before construction ever begins. Interest rates, loan terms, public guarantees, tax abatements, PILOT agreements, and Opportunity Zone incentives all modify the financial calculus facing developers and lenders. These tools adjust projected cash flows, reduce perceived risk, and improve debt-service coverage ratios — often determining in advance which projects will meet underwriting thresholds.

A housing development serving lower-income residents may fail a lender's test not because demand is absent, but because expected returns fall below required benchmarks without substantial subsidy layering. Meanwhile, projects targeting higher-income households frequently appear feasible precisely because public policy has already reduced their exposure to loss through abatements, infrastructure investment, or payment-in-lieu-of-taxes structures.

This dynamic is visible in high-value redevelopment areas such as Paulus Hook and the rest of Downtown Jersey City, where long-term tax abatements and PILOT agreements have materially reshaped project pro formas. In these contexts, feasibility reflects not merely market demand but the cumulative effect of state-enabled financial engineering.

Once feasibility is declared, it becomes destiny. Cities reorganize plans around it. Residents are told that alternatives are unrealistic. The market, it is said, has spoken.

Development Is a Financing Decision

What remains unspoken is that policy helped script the outcome. Financial conditions, incentive structures, guarantees, and regulatory protections shaped which projects could appear viable in the first place. Feasibility is not simply discovered; it is constructed through institutional design.

Even where large, well-resourced institutions intentionally attempt to expand access to housing, the primacy of finance remains evident. In Durham, North Carolina, housing initiatives connected to Duke University revealed that **nearly 80 percent of lower-wage employees interested in homeownership were unable to qualify for mortgages due to credit constraints, even when employer-backed assistance was available.**[1] The binding constraint was not demand, land availability, or stated policy commitment to affordability. It was underwriting.

Only after the university and its partners introduced intensive credit counseling, loan supports, and layered financing mechanisms did homeownership become attainable for some participants.[23] The episode illustrates a broader structural reality: in contemporary urban development, feasibility is less a reflection of social need

---

[1] Meagan M. Ehlenz, Universities and Affordable Housing: Seven Case Studies (Philadelphia: Penn Institute for Urban Research, July 5, 2023), 1-9 https://penniur.upenn.edu/publications/universities-and-affordable-housing-seven-case-studies
[2] Ehlenz, Universities and Affordable Housing, 1-9.
[3] Meagan M. Ehlenz, "'Can You Imagine What's Happened in Durham?': Duke University and a New University–Community Engagement Model," Journal of the American Planning Association 87, no. 1 (2021), 45–61, https://doi.org/10.1080/01944363.2020.1782766

than of institutional arrangements that determine who can access credit on viable terms.

This episode in Durham illustrates a contemporary manifestation of the structural barriers documented by Keeanga-Yamahtta Taylor in Race for Profit.[4] Taylor demonstrates that although post–World War II America saw unprecedented growth in homeownership with 60 percent of Americans owning homes by 1960, African Americans were largely excluded from these gains.[5] Despite migrating in large numbers to urban centers in the North and West, Black families faced overcrowded, dilapidated housing and restricted access to FHA-backed loans and suburban development. Taylor notes that in the 1940s and 1950s, Black homeownership lagged 35–50 percent behind white peers, and African Americans disproportionately lived in homes lacking basic infrastructure such as running water or private bathrooms.[6]

Both historical and contemporary cases illustrate that feasibility is less about demand or need and more about access to institutional credit. Where policies and underwriting structures favor certain borrowers or neighborhoods, those areas attract capital and development, while others — often Black or low-income communities remain constrained.[7] Duke's initiatives reveal that even

---

[4] Keeanga-Yamahtta Taylor, *Race for Profit: How Banks and the Real Estate Industry Undermined Black Homeownership* (Chapel Hill: University of North Carolina Press, 2019) 29.

[5] Taylor, *Race for Profit*, 29.

[6] Taylor, *Race for Profit*, 30.

[7] Christopher E. Herbert, Donald R. Haurin, Stuart S. Rosenthal, and Mark Duda, *Homeownership Gaps Among Low-Income and Minority Borrowers and Neighborhoods*, HUD User Publication (Washington, DC: U.S. Department of Housing and Urban Development, Office of

deliberate and well-resourced interventions must confront deeply embedded structural constraints, whereas Taylor's analysis documents how those constraints were historically constructed and reproduced over time. Collectively, their work highlights that access to borrowing—and the conditions attached to it—plays a decisive role in structuring the geography and equity of urban development.

Historical redlining regimes and contemporary financial constraints together underscore a key structural reality: feasibility is socially and institutionally produced. In neighborhoods such as Downtown Jersey City, Downtown Brooklyn, Downtown Harlem, or Five Points (Denver), the use of PILOT agreements, long-term tax abatements, tax increment financing, and Opportunity Zone incentives demonstrates how policy continues to shape the geography of real estate capital.[89] Duke's experience underscores that even well-intentioned, well-resourced interventions must contend with entrenched financial barriers to create genuine access to housing.

Policy Development and Research, March 2005), 10–14, https://www.huduser.gov/publications/pdf/homeownershipgapsamo nglow-incomeandminority.pdf

[8] U.S. Department of Housing and Urban Development, Opportunity Zones dataset, HUD GIS Open Data, accessed February 22, 2026, https://hudgis-hud.opendata.arcgis.com/datasets/HUD::opportunity-zones/explore?location=28.420892%2C0.315564%2C0

[9] Digital Scholarship Lab, University of Richmond, Mapping Inequality: Redlining in New Deal America, accessed February 22, 2026, https://dsl.richmond.edu/panorama/redlining/map#loc=4/40.4939/-95.8425

Figure 2.1: Historical Redlining in Downtown Jersey City: *This map shows historical redlining patterns in Downtown Jersey City. The majority of this area was shaded in red, labeled as "hazardous" under the 1930s Home Owners' Loan Corporation (HOLC) grading system—a designation that systematically restricted investment and access to credit for residents and businesses.[10] Today, much of Downtown has undergone extensive redevelopment and gentrification, reflecting a significant reversal: the area is largely excluded from federal "opportunity zones" because it is already considered desirable and high-value. By contrasting the historical red shading with present-day redevelopment, the figure highlights the enduring legacies of discriminatory investment practices while illustrating how urban*

---

[10] University of Richmond Digital Scholarship Lab, *Mapping Inequality: Redlining in New Deal America*, redlining map for Hudson County (including Downtown Jersey City), accessed February 22, 2026, https://dsl.richmond.edu/panorama/redlining/map/NJ/HudsonCo/are as#mapview=full&loc=13/40.7086/-74.0249

desirability and capital flows have reshaped formerly marginalized neighborhoods.

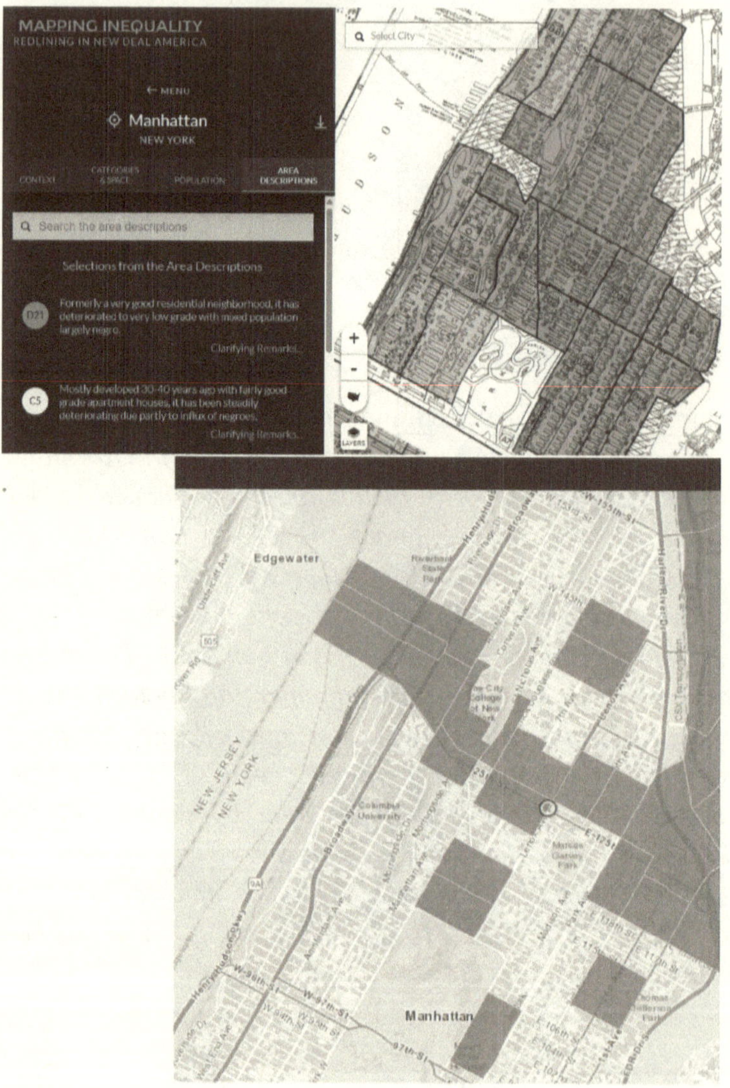

Figure 2.2: Historical Redlining and Contemporary Opportunity Zones in Harlem, Manhattan, New York

Development Is a Financing Decision

This figure overlays Harlem's 1930s HOLC redlining map with the current federal Opportunity Zone designations.[11] *Historically, large portions of Harlem were shaded red, labeled "hazardous," reflecting discriminatory assessments that penalized Black residency regardless of housing quality or neighborhood infrastructure.*[12] *Today, the area contains federally designated Opportunity Zones, highlighting sections targeted for investment and tax incentives.*[13] *The contrast between past and present underscores the enduring impact of racialized credit exclusion while revealing how financial mechanisms now selectively channel capital into neighborhoods once marginalized, reproducing patterns of economic and spatial inequality under a new policy framework.*

---

[11] University of Richmond Digital Scholarship Lab, *Mapping Inequality: Redlining in New Deal America*, redlining map and area descriptions for Manhattan, NY (including Harlem), accessed February 22, 2026, https://dsl.richmond.edu/panorama/redlining/map/NY/Manhattan/area_descriptions#mapview=full&loc=12/40.7897/-73.9625

[12] HUD, Opportunity Zones dataset (HUDGIS Open Data).

[13] U.S. Department of Housing and Urban Development, Opportunity Zones dataset (HUDGIS Open Data).

Figure 2.3: Historical Redlining and Contemporary Opportunity Zones in Downtown Brooklyn

This figure overlays the historical redlining map of Downtown Brooklyn with modern neighborhood boundaries—including DUMBO, Williamsburg, and Bushwick—alongside the current federal Opportunity Zone

designations.[14] *During the 1930s, large portions of these neighborhoods were marked in red, indicating "hazardous" investment risk, a designation that curtailed access to mortgages and constrained capital flows. Today, many of these areas have experienced significant redevelopment, particularly DUMBO and parts of Williamsburg, and are consequently excluded from Opportunity Zones because they are already considered high-value and desirable.*[15][16] *The juxtaposition of past and present highlights the long-term effects of discriminatory investment policies and shows how formerly marginalized neighborhoods have been transformed through market-driven redevelopment, while adjacent areas like Bushwick retain Opportunity Zone status, signaling ongoing potential for incentivized investment.*[17]

Feasibility and Fate in Denver's Five Points and Eastern part of the City

In the case of Denver, Colorado, Five Points section on Denver's East Side occupies a revealing position in the historical geography of American urban development. Long

---

[14] University of Richmond Digital Scholarship Lab, *Mapping Inequality: Redlining in New Deal America*, redlining map for Brooklyn, NY (including DUMBO, Williamsburg, Bushwick), accessed February 22, 2026, https://dsl.richmond.edu/panorama/redlining/map/NY/Brooklyn/areas#mapview=full&loc=12/40.6551/-73.9488

[15] University of Richmond Digital Scholarship Lab, *Mapping Inequality*, Brooklyn, NY map.

[16] U.S. Department of Housing and Urban Development, "Opportunity Zones" dataset, HUDGIS Open Data, accessed February 22, 2026, https://hudgis-hud.opendata.arcgis.com/datasets/HUD::opportunity-zones/explore?location=40.691192%2C-73.996966%2C14

[17] HUD, *"Opportunity Zones"* dataset (HUDGIS Open Data).

recognized as the cultural and commercial center of Black Denver—often referred to as the "Harlem of the West"—the neighborhood was nonetheless subjected to federal redlining practices that laid bare the racial logic embedded in mid-twentieth-century mortgage risk assessment.[18]

Surveyors for the Home Owners' Loan Corporation (HOLC) described Five Points in strikingly ambivalent terms. They acknowledged its solid brick housing stock, stable working-class residents, and adequate infrastructure. Yet these material indicators of neighborhood stability were overshadowed by explicit concern over what they labeled the area's "Negro concentration," which was identified as a primary negative influence on its creditworthiness. Most revealing is the blunt qualification that the neighborhood was, "for a Negro section…very well kept up," followed by the admission that "were it not for the heavy colored population much of it could be rated 'C.'"[19] The implication is unmistakable: the physical condition of the housing stock, the presence of utilities, and the stability of wage-earning households were all deemed insufficient to overcome the presumed financial risk associated with Black residency itself.[20] In other words, the rating penalty was not rooted in the built environment but in a racialized risk calculus

---

[18] Luke Ortiz-Grabe, "A Look Over the Mountain: The Triumph of Denver's Five Points Neighborhood," Senior Division Historical Paper, p. 6, https://clas.ucdenver.edu/nhdc/sites/default/files/attached-files/entry_433.pdf

[19] University of Richmond Digital Scholarship Lab, *Mapping Inequality: Redlining in New Deal America*, "Denver, Colorado, Area Description D13," accessed February 22, 2026, https://dsl.richmond.edu/panorama/redlining/map/CO/Denver/area_descriptions/D13

[20] University of Richmond Digital Scholarship Lab, *Mapping Inequality*, "Denver, Colorado, Area Description D13."

embedded in federal housing policy. The record further acknowledged a bifurcated financial reality, "better class negroes" could sometimes access institutional loans, while others were pushed toward high-fee, high-interest arrangements with industrial operators—foreshadowing the segmented credit markets that would shape the neighborhood's trajectory for decades.[21]

In the contemporary period, Five Points has become a focal point of reinvestment and redevelopment pressures within metropolitan Denver, where rising property values and transit-oriented development have intensified concerns about cultural displacement and the erosion of historically Black residential space. Read alongside the redlining map, the neighborhood's evolution underscores a central theme of this book: urban land long disciplined through racialized credit exclusion is now being selectively revalorized through new financial mechanisms, reproducing structural vulnerability even as the landscape appears to revitalize.

Today, as the East Denver section circumventing the historical Five Points neighborhood experiences renewed investment through Opportunity Zone designations, transit-oriented projects, and market-driven redevelopment, the pattern persists in a structurally analogous form. Feasibility continues to be a product of policy and capital allocation: subsidies, tax abatements, and layered financing create the conditions under which developers perceive projects as viable, while historically marginalized residents confront rising property costs and the risk of displacement. The trajectory of Five Points thus exemplifies the central argument of this section: feasibility is not neutral or

---

[21] *Ibid.*

inevitable; it is actively produced through the intersection of institutional credit, public policy, and racialized valuation of urban land. Historical redlining produced the "fate" of constrained capital decades ago, and contemporary financial instruments now shape which developments are realized and who benefits from them, making the logic of "feasibility" inseparable from the politics of credit and race.

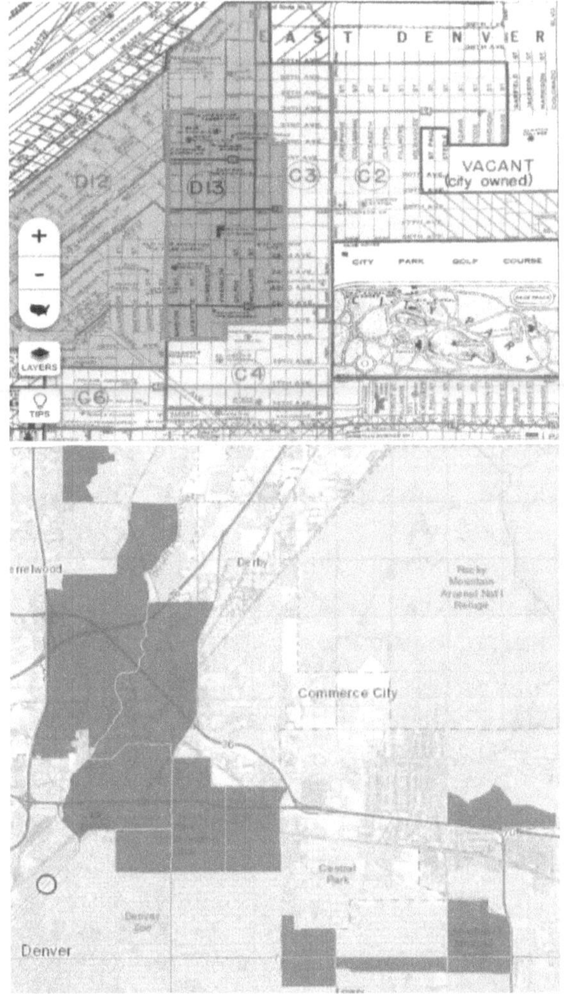

Figure 2.4: Historical Redlining and Contemporary Opportunity Zones in Five Points and East Denver.

This figure juxtaposes the 1930s HOLC redlining map of Five Points with today's federal Opportunity Zone designations.[22] Historically shaded in red and labeled

---

[22] University of Richmond Digital Scholarship Lab, *Mapping Inequality: Redlining in New Deal America*, redlining map and area descriptions

"hazardous" due to its Black population, Five Points was systematically denied access to institutional mortgage credit despite stable housing and infrastructure.[23] The contemporary Opportunity Zone overlay shows the surrounding East Denver area now targeted for investment, illustrating how financial mechanisms continue to shape urban redevelopment[24]. The contrast highlights the enduring legacies of racialized credit policies and the selective revalorization of formerly marginalized neighborhoods.

The Quiet Power of Cheap Credit

If capital is the fuel of development, credit is the engine.

Most urban projects are built on debt. Equity matters, but borrowing determines scale, speed, and survival. When interest rates are low, leverage expands, borrowing costs fall, and development accelerates. When rates rise, projects stall, consolidate, or collapse as debt service burdens increase and financing dries up.

This is how national monetary policy enters the neighborhood through interest rates that shape who can borrow, on what terms, and with what tolerance for risk.

Interest rate decisions made far from any city block shape which projects move forward, which developers survive, and

---

for Denver, CO, accessed February 22, 2026, https://dsl.richmond.edu/panorama/redlining/map/CO/Denver/area descriptions#mapview=full&loc=14/39.763/-104.9511
[23] University of Richmond Digital Scholarship Lab, Mapping Inequality, Denver, CO map and area descriptions.
[24] HUD, Opportunity Zones dataset (HUDGIS Open Data)

which neighborhoods are deemed worthy of investment.[25] Periods of easy credit reward those already positioned to borrow, those with existing assets, institutional relationships, and balance sheets that can absorb leverage. Periods of tightening punish those who are not.

The effects are uneven. Large developers with institutional backing can absorb higher borrowing costs, refinance existing debt, or delay projects until conditions improve. Smaller developers, nonprofit housing providers, and community-based projects cannot. Their margins are thinner, their access to credit more limited, and their timelines less flexible. Over time, development power concentrates not because markets are efficient, but because access to credit is unequal and structurally advantaged.

This uneven access is visible in neighborhoods across the country. In Boston, MA, historically working-class Foundation Black American/ immigrant neighborhoods faced displacement as new lending practices and gentrifying development favored developers with strong institutional backing, while long-time residents struggled to secure mortgage financing. In juxtaposition to the aforementioned point, according to the 2019 study from the National Community Reinvestment Coalition, 21.3% of Boston's "eligible neighborhoods" gentrified between 2013-2017 and the city is ranked as the 3rd most gentrified city in the United States trailing behind San Francisco, CA and Denver, CO.[26]

---

[25] Zain Jaffer, "Surviving High Interest Rates in the Real Estate Industry," Forbes (Forbes Business Council), March 18, 2024, https://www.forbes.com/councils/forbesbusinesscouncil/2024/03/18/surviving-high-interest-rates-in-the-real-estate-industry/

[26] National Community Reinvestment Coalition, *Gentrification and Disinvestment 2020* (Washington, DC: National Community

Roxbury, Boston which is the historically Black section of the city is designated in the study as the most vulnerable to gentrification due the fact that 81% of its residents are renters.[27] Henceforth, areas like Roxbury are vulnerable to economic extraction where the long term and generational residents pay for the development of their neighborhood at the price of economic depravity and displacement.

Additionally, according to the Harvard University Joint Center for Housing Studies, for example, while the number of Black homebuyers statewide increased 40 percent from 2018 to 2021, many were priced out of Boston proper and concentrated in select cities and towns south of the city—Brockton, Randolph, Taunton, and Stoughton.[28] These areas have become important hubs for Black homeownership, yet the concentration also highlights emergent segregation, uneven infrastructure, and the long-term implications for wealth-building and local opportunity. FHA loans played a critical role in enabling these purchases: 40 percent of Black homebuyers statewide relied on FHA-backed mortgages, compared to only 9 percent of white homebuyers.[29] While FHA loans reduce barriers for first-time buyers and those

---

Reinvestment Coalition, June 2020), accessed February 22, 2026, https://ncrc.org/gentrification20

[27] CBS Boston, "Report: Boston Is 3rd 'Most Intensely Gentrified City' in America," *CBS Boston*, July 8, 2020, https://www.cbsnews.com/boston/news/boston-gentrification-study-cities-report/

[28] Harvard Joint Center for Housing Studies, "Discrimination in Home Lending and Appraisals: Challenges for Black Homebuyers in Massachusetts," *JCHS Housing Blog*, accessed February 22, 2026, https://www.jchs.harvard.edu/blog/discrimination-home-lending-and-appraisals-challenges-black-homebuyers-massachusetts

[29] Harvard Joint Center for Housing Studies, "Discrimination in Home Lending and Appraisals."

with lower credit scores, they come with higher long-term costs (mortgage insurance premiums) and face stigmas in competitive markets, limiting access to housing in high-demand areas.[30]

Pittsburgh's Hill District, a historically Black neighborhood, saw public housing transitions and limited access to private credit, which restricted homeownership and small-scale redevelopment.[31] In the Pittsburgh context, the concentration of Black homebuyers in only a small number of suburban municipalities risks reproducing patterns of residential segregation, with significant implications for wealth accumulation and access to local resources. Additionally in Pittsburgh, the Black population declined by roughly 10,500 residents or 13.4 percent between 2010 and 2020, markedly exceeding the city's overall population decrease of 0.9 percent.[32] During this period, median home values in the region increased from $88,000 in 2010 to $149,200 in 2019, a 69.5 percent escalation that has rendered previously attainable housing increasingly inaccessible to

---

[30] Mark Zandi and Cristian deRitis, *The Case for Lower FHA Premiums* (West Chester, PA: Moody's Analytics, January 2015), accessed February 22, 2026, https://www.economy.com/getlocal?q=5cc421dd-4480-4961-b576-2594d0aab92e&app=eccafile

[31] Jared Foretek, "The Story of the Pittsburgh Neighborhood That Inspired 'Fences,'" *Saving Places* (National Trust for Historic Preservation), February 24, 2017, https://savingplaces.org/stories/the-story-of-the-pittsburgh-neighborhood-that-inspired-fences

[32] Charlie Wolfson, "2020 Census: Pittsburgh's Slight Decline Came with 'Massive' Demographic Shifts in 2010s," *PublicSource*, August 13, 2021, https://www.publicsource.org/pittsburgh-allegheny-county-census-2020/ . ("PublicSource" covers local accountability and policy reporting in the Pittsburgh region)

long-term residents.[33] Compounding this pressure, corporate purchasers accounted for approximately one in six single-family home acquisitions in 2020, up from one in nine a decade earlier, further constraining the supply of affordable, quality housing for low- and moderate-income (LMI) Black households and intensifying residential instability.[34]

Black homeownership in Pittsburgh remains disproportionately low. In 2019, only 31.4 percent of Black residents in the metropolitan area owned their homes, compared with 73.0 percent of non-Hispanic white residents and 42.2 percent of Black homeowners statewide.[35] This gap has widened over the last decade, despite an overall decline in regional homeownership, highlighting entrenched structural barriers—including disparities in income, differential access to credit, and gaps in financial education and institutional trust—that systematically limit Black households' ability to secure and sustain homeownership. High-value areas like DUMBO in Brooklyn, NY, Downtown Atlanta, GA, and Manhattan, NY relied heavily on PILOT agreements, Opportunity Zones, and long-term tax abatements to attract investment, concentrating

---

[33] Pittsburgh Community Reinvestment Group, Black Homeownership Report: Taking Stock – *A Decade in Decline for Black Homeownership in Pittsburgh*, (Pittsburgh: Pittsburgh Community Reinvestment Group, March 2022), 1–2, https://www.pcrg.org/black-homeownership-report

[34] Pittsburgh Community Reinvestment Group, *Black Homeownership Report*, 1–2

[35] Pittsburgh Community Reinvestment Group, *Black Homeownership Report*, 7

development in already wealthy areas while excluding lower-income communities from new growth.[36][37]

In further corroboration of these points, according to the U.S. Treasury data, $89 billion flowed through Opportunity Zone funds between 2019-2022 where the wealthiest Americans received over $100 billion in capital gains.[38] Additionally, 85% of the investors average $4.9 million in annual income and 69% of the neighborhoods that were already gentrifying from 2013-2017 either were located in or adjacent to Opportunity Zones.[39] Consistent with the book's argument regarding the entrenchment of racial hierarchies within capitalist development, neighborhoods that later underwent gentrification had an estimated 77% minority population prior to the onset of the process.[40] As previously discussed, the etymology of "gentrification" derives from the concept of the gentry, or "to make noble," which carries an implicit judgment of inferiority regarding the communities already inhabiting these areas. From a geographical and spatial

---

[36] City of Atlanta, *Affordable Housing Strike Force Update* (Atlanta: City of Atlanta, 2024), https://www.atlantaga.gov/home/showpublisheddocument/64358/63873659596500000

[37] Independent Budget Office, *Exemption or Abatement?* Structure of Proposed New 421-a Program Has Implications for All Property Tax Bills (New York: Independent Budget Office, March 2024), https://www.ibo.nyc.ny.us/iboreports/exemption-or-abatement-structure-of-proposed-new-412-a-program-has-implications-for-all-property-tax-bills-march-2024.pdf

[38] National Community Reinvestment Coalition (NCRC), "Opportunity Zones: A Taxpayer-Funded Program That Primarily Benefits Wealthy Investors," accessed February 21, 2026, https://ncrc.org/opportunity-zones-a-taxpayer-funded-program-that-primarily-benefits-wealthy-investors/

[39] NCRC, "Opportunity Zones."

[40] *Ibid.*

context, California, New York, New Jersey and Connecticut lead in planned investments from family offices who serve the financial interests of their wealthy clients.[41]

Similar patterns emerge in Downtown Atlanta, where long-term abatements favor luxury condos and commercial projects over community-oriented housing.[42] Backed by $8.2 billion in public and private investment, projects like Centennial Yards and the South Downtown redevelopment are reshaping large swaths of the district with high-end residential units, hotels, entertainment venues, and office space.[43] Centennial Yards' transformation of the Westside Gulch in Downtown Atlanta has been fueled by sophisticated, large-scale financing. In 2025, D.A. Davidson's Development Finance Group, J.P. Morgan and co-manager Truist Securities secured $575 million in bonds, structured as tax-increment–secured revenue and convertible capital appreciation bonds, to support early-stage development of the $5 billion, 50-acre project.[44] This infusion, combined with additional financing from co-investors including CIM Group and the Atlanta Development Authority, illustrates how large-scale urban redevelopment depends on complex credit arrangements that are inaccessible to smaller developers or local

---

[41] *Ibid.*

[42] Metro Atlanta Chamber, "Downtown Atlanta: A Center of Growth, Investment and Opportunity," accessed February 21, 2026, https://metroatlantachamber.com/downtown-atlanta-a-center-of-growth-investment-and-opportunity/

[43] Metro Atlanta Chamber, "Downtown Atlanta."

[44] Mike Boyd, "Trio Secures $575M for Centennial Yards," *ConnectCRE*, accessed February 21, 2026, https://www.connectcre.com/stories/trio-secures-575m-for-centennial-yards/

homeowners.[45] Although the project promises new residential, commercial, and entertainment spaces, only 20 percent of units are designated as affordable housing, illustrating how financial structuring directs capital toward high-return developments and determines who can access and benefit from urban growth.[46] While the project will deliver 2,600 residential units (20% affordable), hotels, office space, and entertainment venues, the scale and structure of financing exclude smaller developers and local homeowners, reinforcing structural inequality.[47] Public incentives channel credit toward high-return developments, shaping who can participate in urban growth.

In the case of the Jersey Shore in the early 2000s in Wildwood, NJ, over 50 iconic Doo Wop motels were demolished to make way for condominium towers.[48] The surge in redevelopment was enabled by cheap credit and abundant construction financing, which made high-density, high-return projects appear feasible. The redevelopment plan for Wildwood, NJ which was approved by the city's

---

[45] Michael Tobin, "CIM-Backed Revamp of Atlanta Downtown to Tap Muni Market," *Bloomberg*, August 15, 2024, https://www.bloomberg.com/news/articles/2024-08-15/cim-backed-revamp-of-atlanta-downtown-to-tap-muni-market

[46] Mike Boyd, "Trio Secures $575M for Centennial Yards," *ConnectCRE*, accessed February 21, 2026, https://www.connectcre.com/stories/trio-secures-575m-for-centennial-yards/

[47] Bloomberg News, "CIM-Backed Revamp of Atlanta Downtown to Tap Muni Market," *Bloomberg*, August 15, 2024, https://www.bloomberg.com/news/articles/2024-08-15/cim-backed-revamp-of-atlanta-downtown-to-tap-muni-market

[48] Stephanie M. Hoagland, "Preservation Stagnation on the Jersey Shore," National Park Service, accessed February 21, 2026, https://www.nps.gov/articles/000/preservation-stagnation-on-the-jersey-shore.htm

zoner was to allow the motel owners to build up to 25 story condominium developments/resorts and while these projects were underway, the growing inaccessibility of "cheap capital" hindered this process.[49] When the financial crisis hit after 2006, these projects slowed, underscoring that feasibility is contingent on access to capital rather than an inevitable market outcome. Small property owners and historic preservationists, lacking the same financial leverage, were largely excluded from shaping the neighborhood's redevelopment, mirroring structural patterns observed in urban housing markets across the country.

While the aforementioned developments bring new infrastructure, restaurants, and pedestrian improvements, they primarily serve affluent residents and investors, reinforcing existing economic hierarchies. Public incentives and tax abatements channel capital toward these high-value projects, leaving historically Black and/or lower-income neighborhoods largely excluded from the benefits of revitalization. This structural distribution of financial incentives reinforces existing inequities and systematically excludes lower-income and minority communities from participation in urban growth, illustrating that feasibility is as much a policy-constructed condition as a market outcome. What appears as financial discipline is often exclusion—masking hierarchy as prudence and consolidation as neutrality.

Across contexts, Boston, Pittsburgh, Brooklyn, Manhattan, Atlanta and Wildwood from strictly an economic sense, reveal that access to credit and financial incentives is a key

---

[49] Constance Rosenblum, "A Wildwood Makeover," *New York Times*, July 1, 2005, https://www.nytimes.com/2005/07/01/realestate/a-wildwood-makeover.html

mechanism through which urban development reproduces inequality.

In closing, cheap capital is powerful, but its quiet power is structured: it favors those already positioned to benefit while leaving vulnerable communities behind.

When Cities Borrow to Grow

Municipal governments are deeply entangled in this process. Cities borrow to build infrastructure, stabilize budgets, and signal growth to capital markets. Their credit ratings depend on fiscal restraint predictable revenue streams, and the ability to demonstrate future tax capacity.[50] To maintain access to cheap borrowing, cities prioritize projects that promise immediate or near-term fiscal returns, often through rising property values, new construction, or expanded commercial activity.

For instance, as aforementioned, in Downtown Atlanta, the Atlanta Development Authority issued roughly $556 million in municipal bonds to underwrite infrastructure and early-stage costs for the $4.2 billion Centennial Yards redevelopment, leveraging projected future tax revenues from the site.[51] Such bond issues—typically marketed to institutional investors—create financial pathways for large mega projects that smaller

---

[50] Talmon Joseph Smith, *"A Municipal Debt Boom Is Driving Public Projects and Tax Breaks for Investors,"* The New York Times, January 28, 2026,
https://www.nytimes.com/2026/01/28/business/economy/municipal-debt-market.html

[51] CRE Daily Staff and Han Lung, "CIM Taps $556M in Muni Bonds to Fund $4.2B Atlanta Project," *CRE Daily*, August 16, 2024,
https://www.credaily.com/briefs/cim-taps-556-million-dollars-in-muni-bonds-to-fund-4-2-billion-dollar-atlanta-project

developers or community-based entities cannot access. Similarly, cities like Chicago generate hundreds of millions in tax increment financing (TIF) revenues through dozens of TIF districts, using incremental taxes to fund infrastructure and redevelopment at scale.[52] These structured financing mechanisms demonstrate how municipal borrowing channels capital toward high-return projects, shaping not only what is feasible, but who can meaningfully participate in urban growth.[53]

Chicago provides a contemporary example of how these incentives operate in practice. In October 2025, Mayor Brandon Johnson announced a $1 billion TIF surplus for the 2026 fiscal year—a nearly nine-fold increase from the $113 million reported in 2016.[54] TIF districts are designated areas where the growth in property tax revenues is legally earmarked for redevelopment within the district. When revenues exceed project costs, unpledged funds can be declared "surplus" and redistributed to the city, the Chicago Public Schools system, and other local taxing bodies.[55] In 2026, the proposed sweep would allocate

---

[52] Daniel Vesecky, "Understanding Chicago's 2026 Record TIF Surplus," *Civic Federation*, December 1, 2025, https://www.civicfed.org/understanding-chicagos-2026-record-tif-surplus

[53] Vesecky, "Understanding Chicago's 2026 Record TIF Surplus."

[54] Illinois Policy Institute, "Mayor Johnson's Record-Setting $1 Billion TIF Surplus Highlights Issues and Abuse of Chicago's Tax Increment Financing Districts," *Illinois Policy Institute*, December 3, 2025, https://www.illinoispolicy.org/mayor-johnsons-record-setting-1-billion-tif-surplus-highlights-issues-and-abuse-of-chicagos-tax-increment-financing-districts/

[55] Illinois Policy Institute, "Mayor Johnson's Record-Setting $1 Billion TIF Surplus Highlights Issues and Abuse."

$232.6 million to the city and $552.4 million to CPS.[56] While legal and predictable, this practice illustrates how TIFs—originally intended to fund local redevelopment—can be re-purposed to manage broader budgetary pressures.

The Chicago case underscores a structural tension inherent in municipal finance. Growth-oriented financing strategies like TIFs and municipal bonds inherently reward projects that generate near-term fiscal benefits. Long-term strategies focused on affordability, displacement prevention, or reinvestment in existing communities seldom generate equivalent immediate financial returns, despite their potential to produce more durable and equitable social outcomes. The repeated declaration of TIF surpluses demonstrates how incentives harden into routine policy: municipalities systematically redirect funds from localized development toward broader fiscal stability, sometimes delaying or deprioritizing projects within the districts themselves.

Over time, this pattern reveals a fundamental truth: development often becomes a tool for managing debt rather than meeting social need. Cities pursue growth to protect balance sheets, even when that growth exacerbates housing costs, displacement, and long-term fiscal exposure. Chicago's record-setting TIF surpluses are not evidence of corruption; rather, they reflect rational behavior within a legally structured system of incentives. Officials respond predictably to the fiscal architecture they operate within, prioritizing mechanisms that maximize budget flexibility while maintaining creditworthiness.

---

[56] *Ibid.*

Development Is a Financing Decision

In this light, municipal finance is less a reflection of mismanagement than a demonstration of incentive-driven governance. Bond issues, TIF districts, and other structured financing tools channel capital toward high-return projects, shaping urban growth and determining which actors—typically large developers and institutional investors—can participate meaningfully. As these incentives repeat over time, they solidify into policy norms, often producing outcomes that favor growth and financial stability over long-term equity or community-centered development.

Layered Deals and Disappearing Responsibility

By the time a major urban redevelopment project reaches public view, its financing is often already labyrinthine. Private equity sits alongside commercial debt, public subsidies, tax credits, and municipal guarantees. Each layer redistributes risk incrementally, dispersing responsibility across multiple institutions and obscuring clear lines of accountability. The result is a financial architecture that is simultaneously enabling and opaque.

This complexity is often justified as necessary. Without layered financing, many large-scale urban projects—including stadiums, waterfront redevelopments, and mixed-use mega projects—would never proceed. And in many cases, that is true. Layered deals allow cities to leverage limited public resources, attract private capital, and realize ambitious projects that might otherwise remain infeasible.

Yet complexity also serves a second, less visible function: it obscures responsibility. When a project under-performs or produces unintended social costs, it becomes difficult to determine who bears the consequences. Public entities absorb losses through forgone revenue, extended abatements, or future concessions, while private actors retain ownership and capture any remaining upside. Residents and taxpayers are told the outcome was unfortunate, but unavoidable. Neutrality becomes the story. Structure disappears.

The aforementioned case of Chicago offers a clear example. Downtown TIF districts, layered with public subsidies and private investment, generate surpluses that are periodically swept into the city budget. While these mechanisms enable large-scale redevelopment and stabilize municipal finances, they also create accountability gaps. When projects fail to deliver affordable housing or exacerbate displacement, tracing responsibility is nearly impossible: city officials, private developers, and institutional investors share benefits and risks unevenly, leaving the public with the residual social cost.

Layered financing structures, as seen in projects like Atlanta's Centennial Yards or New York City's Hudson Yards, not only concentrate upside for private actors while diffusing risk across public institutions and residents, but they also generate social tensions that catalyze local activism.[57] As Saito's analysis of the L.A. Live redevelopment in Los Angeles demonstrates, the complexity of public–private financing arrangements—combining municipal bonds, tax incentives, and developer equity—both obscures accountability and creates points of leverage for community groups seeking influence through mechanisms

---

[57] Emma G. Fitzsimmons, "Hudson Yards and the New New York," *New York Times*, March 18, 2019, https://www.nytimes.com/2019/03/18/nyregion/newyorktoday/nyc-news-hudson-yards.html

such as Community Benefits Agreements.[58] This dynamic echoes the central insight of Molotch in The City as a Growth Machine: capitalist growth machines prioritize economic expansion and capital accumulation, often at the expense of local communities, yet these very processes produce activists who contest displacement, demand equitable outcomes, and negotiate for social protections.[59] In effect, the opacity and structural incentives of layered urban finance do not merely redistribute fiscal risk—they also shape the terrain of urban politics, producing organized resistance that emerges directly from the contradictions of growth-oriented development.[60]

Another high-profile examples include, New York City's Hudson Yards: The $25□billion project combined tax-exempt bonds, developer equity, tax increment financing (TIF), and extensive city infrastructure investment.[61] Its financing structure dispersed risk across public and private actors, while projected long-term tax revenues were used to justify immediate subsidies.[62] Accountability for rising housing costs, public space management, and infrastructure performance is diffused across multiple city agencies, private developers, and investors.

An aforementioned development was the Los Angeles' L.A. Live / Staples Center redevelopment. This project employed

---

[58] Leland T. Saito, "How Low-Income Residents Can Benefit from Urban Development: The L.A. Live Community Benefits Agreement," *City & Community* 11, no. 2 (2012): 129–50, https://journals.sagepub.com/doi/10.1111/j.1540-6040.2012.01399.x
[59] Saito, "How Low-Income Residents Can Benefit from Urban Development."
[60] *Ibid.*
[61] *Ibid.*
[62] *Ibid.*

a mix of municipal bonds, special district taxes, and private partnerships. While it revitalized downtown and generated entertainment revenue, the layering of deals obscured which entity was responsible for public costs, infrastructure maintenance, and community displacement.

Across these cases, a clear pattern emerges: layered deals concentrate upside for private actors while diffusing downside risk across public institutions and residents. Financial engineering enables mega projects and infrastructure development, but it also systematically obscures who is accountable when social, fiscal, or spatial outcomes deviate from projections.

In this system, incentives are structurally aligned to reward growth and defer responsibility. Municipal actors prioritize creditworthiness and project feasibility, private actors maximize profit, and the public—residents, communities, and taxpayers—bears residual risk. Complexity becomes a tool not just for financing, but for managing perception: failures are framed as neutral or unavoidable, leaving the deeper structural dynamics invisible.

Layered deals, then, are not simply financial instruments, they are mechanisms that enable urban growth while eroding accountability, producing outcomes that serve capital and fiscal stability more than community need.

In this way, layered financing not only shapes who benefits and who bears risk—it also creates the conditions Molotch identifies, where growth-oriented cities simultaneously generate both concentrated capital and grassroots activism contesting the consequences of that growth.

Why Investment Keeps Returning to the Same Places

Some neighborhoods are consistently described as promising. Others remain perpetually risky. This pattern persists even when underlying conditions change.

The reason lies in how risk is remembered.

Lenders and investors rely on historical data shaped by decades of discrimination, redlining, and disinvestment. Neighborhoods denied capital in the past appear risky in the present precisely because they lack prior investment, stable comparables, and established credit histories.[63] The absence of development, is treated not as evidence of exclusion, but as a proof of danger. Risk becomes endogenous: produced by past policy and then cited to justify continued avoidance.

Public intervention can interrupt this cycle, but only if it prioritizes stabilization over speculation. When public tools are used primarily to de-risk extraction—by insulating capital without protecting residents, they accelerate displacement rather than correcting exclusion. These examples are prevalent in Brooklyn, NY, Boston, MA, San Francisco, CA, Jersey City, NJ, Hoboken, NJ, the Western part of South Central, CA and throughout the United States.

Feasibility thus becomes self-reinforcing. Places that already have capital attract more. Places that do not are left behind not because they are inherently risky, but because risk has been institutionally encoded and repeatedly reproduced.

---

[63] Keeanga-Yamahtta Taylor, "Let the Buyer Beware," in Race for Profit: How Banks and the Real Estate Industry Undermined Black Homeownership (Chapel Hill, NC: University of North Carolina Press, 2019; online edition, North Carolina Scholarship Online, January 21, 2021), https://academic.oup.com/north-carolina-scholarship-online/book/38037/chapter-abstract/332596872?redirectedFrom=fulltext

Development Is a Financing Decision

Credit as Governance

To see development as a financing decision is to recognize credit as a form of governance. Decisions about who can borrow, on what terms, and with what protections shape cities as surely as zoning codes, planning commissions, or elections.

These decisions occur far from public scrutiny—in lending committees, bond markets, and regulatory frameworks that operate beyond the reach of most residents. People encounter their consequences only after they are enacted, when rents rise, taxes shift, public services are reallocated, and neighborhoods change.

This distance produces frustration and distrust. It also insulates decision-makers from accountability by framing outcomes as technical, market-driven, or inevitable rather than as the result of policy choices embedded in financial systems.

If financing governs development, then transparency is not optional. It is democratic necessity without which power operates without visibility, and residents are left to absorb outcomes they had no role in shaping.

Conclusion: Changing the Question

When development is framed as planning, debate centers on form. When it is framed as market outcome, debate centers on inevitability. Framing development as financing changes the question entirely.

Who has access to credit?

Who is protected from loss?

Who pays when projections fail?

These questions do not promise consensus. But without them, cities will continue to mistake financial engineering for progress and exclusion for prudence, treating financial feasibility as neutrality rather than as the product of policy choice.

Understanding development as a financing decision does not end conflict. It clarifies it. And clarity is the first condition of responsibility.

CHAPTER 3: The Myth of Private Investment

Private investment is often described as if it were a natural force, something that arrives, withdraws, and reallocates itself according to immutable laws. Cities speak of "attracting" it. Communities are told they must become "competitive" for it. When it fails to appear, blame is assigned not to capital, but to place.

This language grants private investment a peculiar authority. It appears voluntary, apolitical, and external to governance. Public officials present themselves as facilitators rather than participants, clearing obstacles so that capital may flow where it chooses.

But private investment in cities is rarely private, and it is never neutral. In practice, municipal access to low-cost borrowing and favorable credit ratings often depends on demonstrating precisely the kind of tax-generating growth that large private projects promise. It is conditioned by public policy, protected by public institutions, and shaped by decisions that determine where risk is absorbed and where returns are secured.

How Investment Is Made to Appear Natural

The belief that private capital independently selects locations obscures the extensive public architecture that makes those choices possible. Zoning variances, tax abatements, infrastructure upgrades, public land dispositions, loan guarantees, and credit enhancements all shape where capital flows and under what conditions it is willing to enter.[1] These interventions do not merely accompany investment; they actively construct its risk profile. This pattern is well documented in urban political economy and housing scholarship. Studies of federally backed mortgage markets and postwar suburbanization demonstrate that capital flows have long been conditioned by layered public guarantees rather than by purely market-driven site selection.[2] The appearance of spontaneous investment often masks a prior sequence of policy decisions that reduced uncertainty, standardized lending environments, and concentrated public support in geographically selective ways.

Investment does not simply respond to opportunity. It is invited, insured, and protected.

Yet once capital enters a neighborhood, its presence is retroactively framed as validation. *The market*, it is said, *has recognized value*. This logic reverses causality. Public action absorbs uncertainty first —through subsidy, guarantee, and infrastructure—, making subsequent private returns appear inevitable rather than engineered.

The myth persists because it is useful. It allows public actors to claim success without ownership of outcomes, and private

---

[1] Rachel Weber, "Fast Money Builds the Speculative City," in From Boom to Bubble: How Finance Built the New Chicago (Chicago: University of Chicago Press, 2015; Chicago Scholarship Online, 2016), https://doi.org/10.7208/chicago/9780226294513.003.0002

[2] Richard Rothstein, *The Color of Law: A Forgotten History of How Our Government Segregated America* (New York: Liveright, 2017); Keeanga-Yamahtta Taylor, *Race for Profit* (Chapel Hill: University of North Carolina Press, 2019); Matthew Desmond, *Evicted: Poverty and Profit in the American City* (New York: Crown, 2017).

actors to claim independence without accountability for the risks they did not bear.

Morristown's redevelopment trajectory illustrates how municipal borrowing and fiscal strategy can quietly reorganize the geography of growth. Beginning with the Headquarters Plaza project and the construction of the Hyatt Regency Morristown, local officials pursued a downtown-centered development model designed to strengthen the tax base and signal creditworthiness to capital markets particularly in an era when municipal borrowing costs were increasingly sensitive to demonstrated ratable growth and fiscal predictability. When Morristown launched its urban renewal initiative in 1971, the effort was not merely a modernization program but an expression of a fiscal logic that favored large commercial ratables and hospitality developments because they promised predictable short-term revenue streams. During the planning process of the Headquarters Plaza project, Town council and city leaders cited that there would be $1.2 million in ratables generated instead of the $32,000 per year from existing properties.[34] The redevelopment process required substantial public coordination — including land assembly, infrastructure commitments, and zoning accommodations — that effectively reduced risk for private investors while

---

[3] Ronald Smothers, "In New Jersey, Morristown Renewal Still Debated," *New York Times,* June 23, 1985, https://www.nytimes.com/1985/06/23/realestate/in-new-jersey-morristown-renewal-still-debated.html.
[4] Jeffrey Moy, "Downtown vs. The Mall: The Story of Morristown's Headquarters Plaza and Urban Renewal in Morris County," *Morristown Green*, November 2, 2019, https://morristowngreen.com/2019/11/02/downtown-vs-the-mall-the-story-of-morristowns-headquarters-plaza-and-urban-renewal-in-morris-county/

concentrating public exposure in surrounding neighborhoods.[5] The first office tower opened in 1980, the three office towers opened in 1982 and final construction was complete in 1988.[6] The plaza consists of 150,000 square feet dedicated to shopping, a 168 room hotel which includes two restaurants which eventually became the Hyatt Regency, a 10 screen movie theater and a 2,500 car garage and a 40,000 square foot fitness club.[7] In the midst of the amenities of Headquarters Plaza, the urban renewal project rarely attracted people other than the workforce in the newly constructed office buildings even though the plaza succeeded in seasonal outdoor music festivals.[8] The redevelopment displaced existing tenants, leaving the site that later became Headquarters Plaza in Morristown vacant for nearly a decade before construction of the three-tower complex and park commenced in 1981.[9] Historical accounts indicate that the urban renewal clearance associated with Headquarters Plaza displaced more than one hundred families, many from Morristown's historically Black Second Ward near present-day Martin Luther King Avenue.[10] Contemporary demographic patterns suggest the Black residents today comprise roughly 7.5 percent of Morristown's population.[11]

---

[5] Moy, "Downtown vs. The Mall."

[6] *Ibid.*

[7] *Ibid.*

[8] *Ibid.*

[9] *Ibid.*

[10] Chris Connors, "50 Years of Broken Promises and Record Flooding in Morristown," *Morristown Minute*, accessed February 21, 2026, https://morristownminute.town.news/g/morristown-nj/n/41748/50-years-broken-promises-and-record-flooding-morristown

[11] U.S. Census Bureau, *QuickFacts: Morristown town, New Jersey*, accessed February 21, 2026,

Subsequent investment patterns have continued to favor the downtown core and high-value corridors such as Speedwell Avenue, Park Place, and South Street, while adjacent areas experienced comparatively slower capital inflows and persistent infrastructure challenges. The pattern reflects a broader structural dynamic: when municipal fiscal health is tied to expanding ratables and maintaining favorable borrowing conditions, cities rationally privilege projects that maximize assessed value growth. Over time, this incentive structure channels investment toward already-advantaged districts and away from stabilization strategies in historically marginalized neighborhoods. In this sense, Morristown's experience does not represent an aberration or policy failure but rather the predictable outcome of a municipal finance regime in which development functions as a tool of balance-sheet management. As earlier chapters have shown, this dynamic is especially pronounced during periods of cheap credit, when the pressure to convert low borrowing costs into visible growth becomes most acute.

Risk, Return, and the Public Backstop

At the heart of the myth lies a distortion of risk.

Private investors present themselves as bearing uncertainty in exchange for reward. In reality, much of that uncertainty is redistributed through public mechanisms. Municipal bonds finance infrastructure improvements that raise land values and stabilize private assets. Tax increment financing captures future public revenue to stabilize present returns. Subsidized debt lowers borrowing costs and cushions

---

https://www.census.gov/quickfacts/fact/table/morristowntownnewje rsey/PST045225#PST045225

downside exposure.[12] These tools do not eliminate risk; they reposition it.

Credit rating agencies make this logic explicit. According to Moody's Investors Service, long-term obligation ratings evaluate the likelihood that a municipality will meet its financial commitments and the magnitude of potential loss in the event of default.[13] In practice, this framework places extraordinary weight on the stability, predictability, and growth of the local revenue base. Municipal officials therefore operate within a credit regime that quietly rewards policies capable of expanding ratables and penalizes those that do not. What appears publicly as neutral fiscal management is, structurally, a continuous effort to maintain creditworthiness in the eyes of capital markets.

Credit ratings are formally presented as neutral assessments of default risk. Moody's, for example, defines its long-term obligation ratings as opinions regarding the likelihood that a financial obligation will be honored as promised. Yet the capacity to achieve and sustain these ratings is mediated by highly concentrated financial intermediaries. Contemporary market evidence shows that minority-owned underwriting firms continue to handle only a small fraction of municipal bond volume—*roughly five percent*—while large Wall Street institutions dominate senior-manager roles and fee

---

[12] Manuel B. Aalbers, The Financialization of Housing: A Political Economy Approach (London: Routledge, 2016). https://doi.org/10.4324/9781315668666

[13] Moody's Investors Service. *Moody's Rating Symbols and Definitions.* New York: Moody's Investors Service, n.d. https://www.moodys.com/sites/products/productattachments/ap075 378_1_1408_ki.pdf

capture.[14] This disparity is not merely descriptive of market share; it reflects structural differences in balance-sheet capacity, lending relationships, and institutional scale that shape who can meaningfully participate in public finance.

In practice, this means that the same fiscal logic that incentivizes cities like Morristown to pursue high-value downtown development disproportionately favors districts and projects that already align with investor expectations, while historically marginalized communities remain excluded from the financial mechanisms that could sustain growth or stabilization. Public coordination through land assembly, infrastructure commitments, and zoning accommodations—reduces risk for private investors while concentrating exposure elsewhere, yet the intermediaries empowered to translate that stability into market credibility remain overwhelmingly non-diverse. The result is a system in which creditworthiness appears objective but is embedded in a hierarchy that channels both capital and opportunity toward the already advantaged, reinforcing spatial inequality and racialized access to municipal finance.

In this context, creditworthiness appears less as a purely objective measure and more as an outcome embedded within a hierarchically organized financial system. As one minority-owned firm executive noted, increased participation has often meant receiving "more crumbs," underscoring how inclusion initiatives can expand visibility without materially redistributing market power.[15]

---

14 Molly Smith and Danielle Moran, "Up Against Wall Street Bond Giants, Minority Firms Want More," *Bloomberg*, December 17, 2020, https://www.bloomberg.com/news/articles/2020-12-17/up-against-wall-street-bond-giants-minority-firms-want-more

15 Smith and Moran, "Up Against Wall Street Bond Giants."

When projects succeed, returns accrue privately. When they struggle, public entities renegotiate terms, extend abatements, refinance obligations or absorb losses indirectly through reduced services and deferred maintenance. Residents experience these adjustments as austerity, instability, or displacement rather than as financial recalibration.

This asymmetry is not accidental. It reflects a development regime in which capital is systematically shielded while cities compete to appear hospitable to investment. The language of partnership conceals an imbalance of obligation, one in which protection flows upward and exposure flows downward.

The disciplining role of credit markets reinforces these tendencies. Rating agencies such as Moody's Investors Service and S&P Global Ratings explicitly evaluate municipalities based on revenue stability, tax base growth, and expenditure restraint. While rarely framed in spatial terms, these criteria implicitly reward jurisdictions that can demonstrate continuous appreciation in high-value districts. The result is a subtle but powerful feedback loop: cities seeking favorable borrowing costs are structurally encouraged to privilege developments most likely to expand near-term ratables, even when alternative investments might produce more durable social outcomes.

Why Capital "Avoids" Certain Neighborhoods

Investment patterns are often explained through the language of risk. Certain neighborhoods, typically low-income and disproportionately Black or otherwise marginalized, are described as uncertain, unstable, or unproven.

The Myth of Private Investment

But this risk is not intrinsic. It is historical.

Decades of redlining, disinvestment, urban renewal as in the case of Morristown among several cases nationally, displacement and exclusion from credit markets produced the very conditions now cited to justify avoidance.[16] Neighborhoods denied mortgage lending, insurance, and public investment lack the transaction histories and comparable sales that contemporary underwriting relies upon. Absence of data is misread as evidence of danger, rather than as proof of past neglect. Public withdrawal creates the conditions that private capital later declines to enter.

When investment finally arrives, it is often speculative rather than stabilizing. Capital seeks appreciation, not repair as short-term gains rather than long-term continuity. Longtime residents are recast as obstacles to growth rather than beneficiaries of reinvestment, their presence treated as friction rather than as value. This case underscores the central argument of Chapter 3: what appears as voluntary, neutral private investment is in fact meticulously structured by public policy, municipal credit incentives, and financial intermediaries—conditions that systematically favor already advantaged districts while reproducing racial and spatial inequities in historically marginalized neighborhoods.

The market does not discover neighborhoods. It revisits them on terms shaped by power, history, and the selective memory of financial systems.

---

[16] Meizhu Lui, Bárbara J. Robles, Betsy Leondar-Wright, Rose M. Brewer, and Rebecca Adamson, The Color of Wealth: The Story Behind the U.S. Racial Wealth Divide (New York: The New Press, 2006), https://doi.org/10.2307/jj.25291679. 73-130.

The State as Silent Partner

Despite the rhetoric of privatization, the state remains deeply embedded in urban investment. Its role has not diminished; it has shifted.

Rather than acting as direct builder or provider, the state now functions as guarantor, risk manager, and value-creator for private capital.[17] Through credit enhancement, land assembly, regulatory flexibility, and fiscal backstopping, public institutions shape investment conditions while minimizing direct responsibility for outcomes. These interventions are selective, targeted toward projects that align with growth narratives and revenue expectations rather than towards meeting social need.

This arrangement allows officials to claim fiscal discipline while expanding exposure. Because many commitments take the form of contingent liabilities—guarantees, abatements, future revenue pledges—they remain politically invisible until failure occurs. When projects falter, public responsibility is framed as unfortunate necessity or economic realism rather than as the predictable result of prior policy choices.

The result is a form of governance that operates through markets without being accountable to them—exercising power indirectly while insulating itself from democratic scrutiny.

---

[17] David Harvey, "The Neoliberal State," in *A Brief History of Neoliberalism* (Oxford: Oxford University Press, 2005; online edition, Oxford Academic, November 12, 2020), https://doi.org/10.1093/oso/9780199283262.003.0007

For example, Morristown's redevelopment of Headquarters Plaza and the construction of the Hyatt Regency exemplifies the state's silent yet decisive role in shaping urban investment.[18] The municipal government coordinated land assembly, zoning adjustments, and infrastructure commitments, effectively reducing private risk and creating conditions favorable to high-value commercial and hospitality development. Public officials framed these interventions as standard fiscal management, yet the long-term social consequences—displacement of over one hundred families from the historically Black Second Ward, the rechanneling of investment toward downtown corridors like Speedwell Avenue, Park Place, and South Street, and the concentration of fiscal exposure in surrounding neighborhoods—were externalized onto residents rather than recognized as a predictable outcome of policy.[19] Through these mechanisms, the city functioned as a guarantor, risk manager, and value creator for private capital, illustrating the asymmetry described in this section: public financial support enabled private profit while minimizing political visibility and accountability, thereby reinforcing a governance model that exercises power indirectly through market facilitation rather than direct service provision.[20]

---

[18] John Holl, "In Morristown, a Time of Change and Growing Pains," *New York Times*, September 29, 2002, https://www.nytimes.com/2002/09/29/nyregion/in-morristown-a-time-of-change-and-growing-pains.html

[19] PublicSq Staff, "A History of Flooding and Broken Promises in Morristown Black Community," PublicSq, accessed February 21, 2026, https://www.publicsq.org/latest-articles/a-history-of-flooding-and-broken-promises-in-morristown-black-community

[20] PublicSq Staff, "A History of Flooding and Broken Promises in Morristown Black Community."

Financial Discipline as Moral Language

Private investment is often defended through the language of discipline. Markets, it is said, impose efficiency. They reward seriousness and punish excess. This framing moralizes exclusion by presenting market outcomes as deserved rather than as structured.

A contemporary parallel to this dynamic can be found along Washington, D.C.'s U Street Corridor.[21] Historically a hub of Black-owned businesses and known as "Black Broadway," the corridor has undergone intense gentrification over the past several decades.[22] Longtime residents, such as Gregory Adams, have organized through groups like Black Neighbors of 1617 U Street to oppose the D.C. Office of Planning's upzoning proposals, which would permit the construction of a 10-story mixed-use building in place of the four-story limit.[23] Their objections were centered on housing affordability, displacement risks, and insufficient community engagement were often characterized in official and developer rhetoric as obstructing "growth" or resisting private investment. As Adams observed, many long-term residents left not by choice but due to economic necessity, illustrating how speculative capital converts neighborhoods into sites of profit while framing opposition as irrational or anti-progressive. Local historians and advocates have emphasized that meaningful protections for affordable

---

[21] Sam P.K. Collins, "The U Street Corridor: Past Glory, Present-Day Questions," *The Washington Informer*, February 20, 2026, https://www.washingtoninformer.com/u-street-housing-affordability-concerns/

[22] Collins, "The U Street Corridor."

[23] *Ibid.*

housing must be implemented before new development begins; without them, inclusionary zoning and temporary affordability requirements often fail to prevent displacement over time. This example mirrors the structural pattern seen in Morristown: the state and planning authorities facilitate private investment through selective policy interventions while framing community-led concerns as obstacles to market efficiency, thus moralizing capital accumulation and obscuring the social costs of redevelopment.

Projects that cannot attract private capital are described as irresponsible. Communities that resist market-driven redevelopment are portrayed as irrational or anti-growth.

Public spending without private leverage is labeled as wasteful, even when it addresses clear social need.

But discipline is unevenly applied. Large institutions receive patience, flexibility and restructuring when conditions shift. Small developers, nonprofit housing providers and community-based projects face inflexible standards and immediate penalties.[24] What is framed as neutral market logic often reflects hierarchy rather than efficiency privileging scale, political access, and balance-sheet strength over public value.

Discipline becomes a justification rather than an explanation, a moral language that obscures power while naturalizing unequal outcomes.

When Growth Replaces Development

---

[24] Susan S. Fainstein, "The Just City," *International Journal of Urban Sciences 18*, no. 1 (2014): 1–18, https://doi.org/10.1080/12265934.2013.834643

The elevation of private investment reshapes the meaning of development itself. Growth becomes the metric. Rising property values substitute for improved living conditions. Construction volume replaces stability as evidence of success, even when underlying insecurity deepens.

This shift narrows political imagination. Policies that do not immediately attract capital are dismissed as unrealistic or fiscally irresponsible. Long-term public investment without private partnership is treated as naïve, regardless of its potential to produce durable social and economic outcomes.

Development becomes less about improving lives and more about signaling momentum. Cities chase visibility instead of resilience, prioritizing projects that demonstrate activity and confidence over those that build continuity, affordability, and long-term stability. From Morristown's downtown towers to U Street's partial upzoning, cities repeatedly elevate the appearance of growth over the lived realities of residents primarily of color or of lower socio-economic status. In each case, development becomes shorthand for market activity, signaling momentum to investors rather than delivering durable social and economic outcomes to communities.

Conclusion: Demystifying the Market

The myth of private investment persists because it simplifies responsibility. It allows inequality to be explained as outcome rather than as choice. Such a narrative casts public subsidy as unavoidable and displacement as an incidental harm, rather than as a foreseeable result of deliberate policy choices. Morristown's downtown redevelopment and U Street's contested upzoning both demonstrate how the mechanisms of investment — from tax incentives to credit guarantees — systematically prioritize growth over social stability.

Demystifying this myth does not require rejecting private capital. It requires naming the conditions under which capital operates and the protections that make its participation possible. Investment flows where it is protected, rewarded, and stabilized — through public guarantees, regulatory accommodation, and fiscal support. When cities acknowledge this, they gain leverage: they can negotiate terms, set conditions, and align investment with public purpose. When they deny it, they surrender agency and accept market outcomes as fate rather than as governance.

The question is not whether private investment should play a role in development. It already does. The question is whether cities will continue to treat it as destiny — privileging rising property values and visible construction over resident stability and equitable outcomes — or whether they will reclaim development as deliberate policy, ensuring that growth is matched by social responsibility.

Part II: MONEY MOVES NEIGHBORHOOD

CHAPTER 4: Public Risk, Private Reward

Every development deal tells a story about risk. It identifies what might go wrong, who will absorb that uncertainty, and under what conditions failure will be tolerated. Official narratives suggest that private investors shoulder this burden in exchange for profit. Public actors, by contrast, are portrayed as cautious stewards, intervening only to correct market gaps or facilitate otherwise unviable projects.

In practice, the opposite is often true.

Urban development in the contemporary United States is structured around the systematic transfer of risk from private capital to public institutions and, ultimately, to residents. Financial exposure is absorbed through public guarantees, foregone revenue, and service trade-offs, while private actors retain ownership, control, and the bulk of potential returns. This chapter argues that contemporary urban development functions as a risk-transfer regime embedded within municipal finance.

How Risk Enters the Public Ledger

Public risk rarely appears as a single line item. It accumulates through layered commitments: tax abatements that reduce future revenue, infrastructure spending justified by projected growth, subsidized loans that prioritize repayment over public benefit, and guarantees designed to stabilize investor expectations.[1] Individually, these tools

---

[1] Kwame Boadi, Making Sense of the District's Tax Abatement Dollars: Nine Questions to Consider (Washington, DC: *DC Fiscal Policy Institute,*

appear limited and manageable. Collectively, they create long-term fiscal exposure that is difficult to track, quantify, or reverse.

Each intervention is framed as prudent, conditional, and temporary. Taken together, they form a parallel balance sheet, one composed of contingent liabilities and foregone revenues that rarely appears in public debate, budget hearings, or accountability frameworks.

Municipalities accept these exposures because they are told there is no alternative. To refuse is to appear anti-growth, anti-business, or fiscally irresponsible. Participation in the development economy is framed as compulsory, and risk becomes its entry fee.

But unlike private firms, cities cannot walk away from loss. They cannot liquidate neighborhoods, dissolve school systems, or abandon residents without consequence. Their liabilities are political and social, not merely financial and they persist long after individual projects have failed or capital has moved on.

One way to see the transfer of risk from private actors to public institutions is through municipal budgets themselves. In cities like Atlanta, expenditures on housing and community development are dwarfed by allocations to economic development, debt service, and public safety.

For example, in the city of Atlanta, the City Council recently passed a $3 billion budget for the Fiscal Year of 2026 and according to the Proposed General Fund Expenditures, the top three expenditures will first go to the Department of

---

December 14, 2011), https://www.dcfpi.org/wp-content/uploads/2015/12/2011-tax-abatement-paper-final.pdf

Aviation with a proposed amount of $419,469,633, the Department of Police with a proposed amount of $361,000,836 and the Department of Watershed Management with the amount of $342,689,632.[2] Additionally, of the 27 departments of Atlanta's budget allocations, the Department of Finance is ranked #11 where this department will receive $28,357,852 according to the budget proposal where the majority of the expenditures were allocated to salary related expenditures and even though there isn't a numerical value under the *Debt Service* designation, $4,973,532 is proposed to get allocated to *Other Financing Uses* and an additional $12,409,930 are proposed to be allocated to *Other Expenses*.[34]

Not to mention, the Department of Grants and Community Development is ranked #22 in Atlanta's proposed budget with a proposed amount of only $3,109,174! The proposed budget allocations in Atlanta plays an integral role in explaining why White Atlanta families have a median household income of $83,722–three times higher than Black families' median income of $28,105.[5] Hence, as of 2022, Atlanta has the highest income inequality in the country.[6]

---

[2] ATLbudget: the People's Guide to the City of Atlanta's Budget," *ATLbudget*, accessed February 20, 2026, https://atlbudget.org/
[3] *ATLbudget*.
[4] City of Atlanta, *Fiscal Year 2026* Operating Budget, FY 2026 (Atlanta: City of Atlanta, 2025), 199–203, https://www.atlantaga.gov/home/showpublisheddocument/65298#page=199
[5] Kendall Glynn, "White Atlanta Families Have 46 Times More Wealth Than Black Ones. How Do We Fix That?" *Atlanta Civic Circle*, January 17, 2024, https://atlantaciviccircle.org/2024/01/17/atlanta-racial-wealth-gap-solutions/
[6] Dylan Jackson, "Atlanta Has the Highest Income Inequality in the Nation, Census Data Shows," *The Atlanta Journal-Constitution*,

Additionally, the city of Atlanta which is classified as "The Black Mecca" has a staggering disparity where the median net wealth for the White population is $238,355 and the median Black wealth is $5,180 henceforth, the white wealth in Atlanta is 46 times more than Black households.[7] Atlanta has experienced a declining Black population, which comprised 52% of the city in 2018 and currently represents approximately 48% of residents. More than one-third of Black households in Atlanta have zero net worth, compared with 20% of Hispanic households, 13% of White households, and 11% of Asian households.[8]   When we analyze the revenue of Atlanta, the majority of the city's earnings are generated from property taxes which account for $388 million or 39.8% of the budget, secondarily, the local options sales tax which consists of 15.9% of the city's revenue and public utility, alcohol beverage and other taxes consisting of 15.1% of the city's revenue.[9]

As noted previously, Atlanta recently approved up to $1.9 billion in tax incentives to support redevelopment at the site of the Centennial Yards project, a $5 billion mixed-use

---

November 28, 2022, https://www.ajc.com/news/investigations/atlanta-has-the-highest-income-inequality-in-the-nation-census-data-shows/YJRZ6A4UGBFWTMYICTG2BCOUPU/

[7] Atlanta Wealth Building Initiative, *Building a Beloved Economy: A Baseline and Framework for Building Black Wealth in Atlanta*, (Atlanta: Atlanta Wealth Building Initiative, 2023), 7–17, https://buildblackwealth.info/2023/10/AWBI-BuildingABelovedEconomy-Final.pdf

[8] Atlanta Wealth Building Initiative, Building a Beloved Economy, 7–17.

[9] Center for Civic Innovation, *FY 2026 Organizer's Guide to the City of Atlanta Budget* (Atlanta: Center for Civic Innovation, 2025), 4, https://atlbudget.org/wp-content/uploads/2025/05/FY2026-Organizers-Guide-to-the-City-of-Atlanta-Budget.pdf

development led by the CIM Group. In addition, the city authorized the sale of $557 million in government bonds to subsidize construction.[10] Public funding often cushions private projects and stabilizes investor returns, yet investment in resident security—through affordable housing, social services, and community preservation—remains comparatively limited. Municipal budgets thus operate as explicit ledgers of risk allocation: public dollars protect private profits, while residents absorb the consequences when projections fail. Atlanta provides a clear illustration of this dynamic.

If municipal resources in Atlanta—sometimes called "The Black Mecca"—were systematically directed, in conjunction with universities, financial-sector underwriters (including banks and primary dealers of the Federal Reserve), private investors, and federal programs, toward populations in need of institutional support, financing, education, and infrastructure repair, racial and class disparities could likely be reduced. This is not intended to assign blame to local politicians or bureaucrats; rather, it demonstrates how private capital leverages public structures to generate economic gain through mechanisms such as PILOT agreements, municipal bond financing, tax incentives, and other forms of structured investment.

In this framework, the state functions as a fortification apparatus, protecting assets while shifting development risks onto residents, who bear the costs through taxation,

---

[10] Zachary Hansen, "Centennial Yards Draws from Atlanta Incentives to Finance New Construction," *The Atlanta Journal-Constitution*, June 20, 2024, https://www.ajc.com/news/business/centennial-yards-draws-from-atlanta-incentives-to-finance-new-construction/B5SYVBY6L5GE3CRRPSQFHLI6ZM/

displacement, and strained public services. Economically marginalized communities face particularly high opportunity costs when public funds are diverted away from initiatives that could empower both residents and the broader urban ecosystem. Atlanta's case exemplifies how the design of public-private partnerships and financing mechanisms structures not only capital flows but also the distribution of risk and social benefit within the city.

The Asymmetry of Protection

When development performs well, the structure is clear. Investors receive returns. Property values rise. Cities claim success through increased visibility, rising assessments and selective revenue gains.

When development underperforms, protections activate.

Debt is restructured. Abatement periods are extended. Performance benchmarks are revised. Public agencies renegotiate rather than enforce.[11] These adjustments are rarely framed as bailouts. Instead, they are described as flexibility, pragmatism, or economic realism, necessary accommodations to preserve investor confidence and project viability.

Residents, however, receive no such protections. Rent increases triggered by speculative investment are not paused when projections fail. Property tax reassessments are not delayed because promised amenities did not materialize. Displacement is not reversed when developments fall short of public benefit claims. Loss is treated as final at the

---

[11] Manuel B. Aalbers, "Financialization and Housing: Between Globalization and Varieties of Capitalism," in *The Financialization of Housing: A Political Economy Approach* (London: Routledge, 2016).

household level, even as it remains negotiable at the institutional one.

The system is resilient, but only upwards.

Risk as a Political Choice

Risk is often presented as technical henceforth something managed by experts and modeled through projections. This framing disguises its political nature by treating distributional consequences as neutral outputs rather than as deliberate choices.

Deciding to guarantee a loan rather than fund public housing directly is a political choice. Choosing to underwrite market-rate development while austerity governs social services is a political choice. Prioritizing investor confidence over resident stability is a political choice about whose security matters and whose can be treated as flexible.

Yet these decisions are rarely debated as such. They are embedded within financial instruments, delegated to quasi-public authorities, and justified through the language of inevitability, expertise, and market necessity. Politics does not disappear; it is displaced, removed from public deliberation and reintroduced as technical constraint.[12]

By the time consequences emerge, responsibility has already diffused.

Why Austerity Follows Development

---

[12] Ananya Roy, Wendy Larner, and Jamie Peck, "Book Review Symposium: Jamie Peck (2010) Constructions of Neoliberal Reason," Progress in Human Geography 36, no. 2 (2012): 273–81, https://doi.org/10.1177/0309132511413734

Paradoxically, cities that pursue aggressive development strategies often experience intensified austerity. This is not coincidence; it is a structural outcome.

Public resources committed to stabilizing private projects reduce fiscal flexibility. Future revenue streams are pledged in advance through debt service, abatements, and earmarked tax flows. When economic conditions shift, interest rates rise, demand softens, capital retreats—cities face constrained budgets without corresponding control over outcomes or the ability to unwind prior commitments.[13]

Austerity is then framed as discipline rather than consequence. Cuts to public services are justified as fiscal necessity, even as development subsidies remain politically untouchable. Budget shortfalls are attributed to spending excess rather than to the cumulative exposure created by prior growth strategies.

Residents are told that sacrifice is unavoidable. The same logic is never applied to capital.

The Geography of Exposure

Public risk is not evenly distributed across cities. It concentrates in neighborhoods already marked by vulnerability.

Projects in marginalized areas are often more heavily subsidized, justified through the language of revitalization and opportunity. Yet these same areas are least equipped to absorb failure. When promised benefits do not materialize, residents face displacement without replacement, disruption

---

[13] Mark Setterfield, review of *Austerity: The History of a Dangerous Idea*, by Mark Blyth, Eastern Economic Journal 44 (2018): 335–36, https://doi.org/10.1057/eej.2014.57

without repair, and loss without recourse. The downside of experimentation is localized, even when the upside is mobile.

Risk flows downward—geographically and socially.

This pattern reflects what political economists describe as racialized exposure: communities historically excluded from wealth accumulation are repeatedly positioned as buffers for systemic instability.[14] Development does not correct this imbalance. More often, it institutionalizes it, using the language of inclusion to justify the concentration of financial risk in places least able to bear it.

Morristown, New Jersey

Morristown's downtown redevelopment highlights the public absorption of risk while private actors retain the financial upside. Rather than relying on Tax Increment Financing, the town employed PILOT agreements (Payments in Lieu of Taxes) and tax breaks to incentivize private development. For example, the Morris Street 2015 Urban Renewal project, an 85-unit residential development with affordable and special-needs units, received a 25-year PILOT agreement, lowering the property tax obligation in exchange for construction commitments.[15] The town's council justified the arrangement as meeting pressing housing needs, yet it simultaneously shifted fiscal exposure

---

[14] Melanie T. Liu, Thomas Shapiro, Tatjana Meschede, and Laura Sullivan, The Color of Wealth: The Story Behind the U.S. Racial Wealth Divide (New York: The New Press, 2019), 73–130.

[15] Jessie Gomez, "Morristown OKs Tax Break for Residential Project with Special Needs Units," *Morristown Daily Record*, August 18, 2021, https://www.dailyrecord.com/story/news/2021/08/18/apartments-morristown-nj-tax-deal/8178020002/

onto the municipality while guaranteeing long-term certainty and profitability for the developer.

Historical patterns echo the earlier Headquarters Plaza redevelopment: large-scale commercial projects in Morristown were prioritized for their potential to generate immediate ratables, while surrounding historically Black neighborhoods—such as the Second Ward—experienced displacement, low homeownership rates, and slower infrastructure investment. These fiscal arrangements illustrate how public institutions can appear neutral while effectively underwriting private returns, concentrating both risk and reward along racialized and geographic lines. Morristown illustrates that even in smaller suburban municipalities, development finance redistributes risk in ways structurally similar to larger metropolitan markets.

Chicago, Illinois

In Chicago, as mentioned previously, Tax Increment Financing (TIF) districts are a primary tool for channeling public risk into private development.[16] TIF districts divert future property tax revenue from existing public services to subsidize development in designated areas. This has been particularly visible in neighborhoods like Bronzeville and Pilsen, where TIF subsidies supported large commercial and

---

[16] City of Chicago, *Tax Increment Financing (TIF) Program Guide 2020* (Chicago: City of Chicago Department of Planning and Development, 2020), https://www.chicago.gov/content/dam/city/depts/dcd/general/2020_tif_program_guide.pdf

residential developments.[17][18][19][20] While investors receive secure returns and cities gain potential long-term economic growth, critiques note that the original communities often see minimal improvements in housing stability, and public schools and social services experience revenue reductions as a result.

This unevenness gives TIF its distinctly geographic character. The financial upside of redevelopment is mobile and citywide, but the fiscal and social exposure remains locally concentrated. Neighborhoods targeted for revitalization absorb the disruption associated with rising land values, speculative pressure, and service strain, even when promised community benefits materialize only partially or belatedly. In this sense, Chicago's TIF landscape illustrates how the risks of development are not merely economic—they are spatially managed.

The 2026 Protecting Chicago Budget highlights the scale of this dynamic. With the largest TIF surplus in the city's history, exceeding \$1 billion, the city is able to channel significant resources toward both development incentives and public programs.[21] Mayor Brandon Johnson framed this

---

[17] City of Chicago, *TIF District Programming 2021-2025* (Chicago: City of Chicago, Department of Planning and Development), 17, https://www.chicago.gov/content/dam/city/depts/dcd/tif/projections/TIF_District_Programming_2021_2025.pdf

[18] City of Chicago, *TIF District Programming 2021-2025*, 24.

[19] City of Chicago, *TIF District Programming 2021-2025*, 69.

[20] City of Chicago, *TIF District Programming 2021-2025*, 177-79.

[21] City of Chicago, *"Mayor Brandon Johnson Presents the Protecting Chicago Budget Proposal for Fiscal Year 2025,"* press release, October 16, 2025, City of Chicago Office of the Mayor, https://www.chicago.gov/city/en/depts/mayor/press_room/press_releases/2025/october/budget-proposal-2025.html

surplus as a means to safeguard essential services, including Chicago Public Schools, the Chicago Park District, and City Colleges, at a time when federal support was constrained.[22] This demonstrates that TIFs, while primarily designed to stabilize private investment, can be leveraged to protect vulnerable populations—but only when political leadership explicitly prioritizes these outcomes.

Beyond TIFs, the budget introduces new progressive revenue measures aimed at shifting risk back toward wealthier actors. Taxes on large corporations, Big Tech companies, and luxury items such as yachts fund mental health care, community safety programs, and social services that directly benefit residents who might otherwise bear the consequences of speculative investment. Innovative initiatives, like the Social Media Amusement & Responsibility Tax (SMART), provide $31 million for youth mental health clinics, illustrating how fiscal instruments can be structured to mitigate social exposure while sustaining growth.[23]

This approach underscores a key insight from urban finance: the distribution of risk and reward is a political choice, not an inevitable outcome of market forces. In Chicago, TIF districts and related fiscal policies protect investors and incentivize private development, but the city can selectively reclaim risk and direct resources toward public purpose. Programs funded through surplus TIF revenues and new taxes reveal that cities retain leverage to align development with social goals—yet the benefits are contingent on explicit policy design and sustained political will. Without such

---

[22] City of Chicago, *"Mayor Brandon Johnson Presents the Protecting Chicago Budget Proposal."*
[23] *Ibid.*

interventions, the original residents of subsidized neighborhoods continue to experience displacement, reduced service capacity, and precarious stability, even as development proceeds.

For example, the rapid expansion and deepening reliance on TIF also has profound implications for neighborhood-level stability. In Pilsen, long-standing residents have actively opposed proposals to expand the neighborhood's TIF district, arguing that such expansion would accelerate gentrification, drive up property taxes, and displace families who can no longer afford to live there.[24] Survey data from the 25th Ward indicates that roughly 80 percent of neighbors opposed the proposed expansion, with many citing fears that TIF-driven development subsidizes outside investors while offering little long-term benefit to the community.[25] In the face of these concerns, resident-led campaigns have pushed for alternatives that would invest TIF revenues directly into affordable housing and community stabilization rather than further entrenching speculative growth.[26]

This pattern reinforces the argument that public financial tools do not operate evenly across space. While TIFs are justified as mechanisms to eliminate "blight" and spur redevelopment, their actual deployment often fuels rising property values, increased rent pressure, and uneven distribution of public revenue with outcomes that

---

[24] Alex V. Hernandez, "Neighbors Overwhelmingly Reject Expanding Pilsen TIF, Survey Shows," *Block Club Chicago*, August 15, 2025, https://blockclubchicago.org/2025/08/15/neighbors-overwhelmingly-reject-expanding-pilsen-tif-survey-shows/

[25] Hernandez, "Neighbors Overwhelmingly Reject Expanding Pilsen TIF

[26] Pilsen Alliance, "NO Pilsen TIF Expansion!," July 15, 2024, https://www.thepilsenalliance.org/news-and-events/no-pilsen-tif-expansion

disproportionately affect historically marginalized neighborhoods even as investors and developers reap structured returns. In Chicago's case, the expansion of tax increment capture and the resistance it provokes reveal how risk and failure are not simply geographic accidents but politically mediated distributions of public exposure and private reward.

Even so, Chicago's experience reinforces a central insight of the geography of failure: risk is rarely eliminated; it is redistributed. TIF districts and related fiscal instruments stabilize investor expectations while concentrating uncertainty within specific neighborhoods. Corrective policies can mitigate these effects, but they do not automatically undo the localized pressures created by so called "market-oriented redevelopment." Without sustained intervention, communities in subsidized districts continue to experience displacement pressures, constrained service capacity, and heightened precarity, even as aggregate indicators of growth improve.

Stability for Whom?

Development policy often invokes stability: stable tax bases, stable investment climates, stable growth trajectories.

But stability is selectively defined.

Investor stability is actively protected through guarantees, concessions, and risk mitigation, whereas resident stability—including housing security, community continuity, and affordability—is treated as secondary, conditional, or merely aspirational. When the interests conflict with one another, policy consistently prioritizes investor protections over community needs.

This is not a failure of values. It is a revelation of priorities and of the institutional arrangements that determine whose stability is treated as essential and whose is treated as expendable.

Conclusion: Naming the Transfer

Urban development today operates less as a partnership than as a redistribution mechanism, one that channels risk downward while consolidating reward upward.

Naming this transfer does not require rejecting markets or capital. It requires acknowledging that current arrangements are neither neutral nor inevitable. They are structured choices embedded in financial policy, institutional incentives, and governance frameworks that determine how risk and reward are allocated.

Until cities confront how risk is distributed—and who is expected to live with the consequences—development will continue to generate growth without security, investment without trust, and prosperity without inclusion.

The next question, then, is not whether public risk exists. It is whether cities can reclaim it as a tool for public purpose rather than as a backstop for private protection.

CHAPTER 5: Risk is Never Eliminated—Only Moved

From Financial Management to Neighborhood Consequence

Modern urban development is routinely rationalized as risk management. Capital flows are modeled, projections stress-tested, and governance structures arranged to stabilize outcomes. Public officials emphasize minimizing fiscal exposure; investors emphasize hedging uncertainty. The rhetoric implies that risk can be neutralized—yet, systemic and social risks persist, often disproportionately borne by residents.

Risk is not eliminated in contemporary urban development; it is redistributed. It moves across institutions, across balance sheets, and ultimately across social boundaries, away from capital and toward public entities and residents with the least capacity to absorb loss. Financial instruments may stabilize projects on paper, but they often externalize volatility onto neighborhoods through rising costs, service reductions, and displacement.

Understanding this movement is essential to understanding why development repeatedly produces instability at the neighborhood level even when projects appear fiscally sound. What looks like prudence in accounting terms can translate into precarity in lived experience.

The Illusion of Risk Management

At the top of the financial system, risk is treated as a technical problem. Central banks adjust interest rates to cool inflation or stimulate growth. Capital markets price uncertainty through spreads, premiums and diversification strategies. Municipal governments adopt increasingly sophisticated debt instruments to smooth fiscal cycles and manage volatility.

Each layer claims control.

Yet these mechanisms do not neutralize risk. They reorganize it. What appears as stability at one level often requires volatility at another. Inflation control may slow local investment. Credit tightening may stabilize markets while destabilizing housing access. The capacity to manage risk is itself unevenly distributed—concentrated among institutions with liquidity, scale, and political leverage.[1]

Cities, by contrast, occupy an intermediate position. They are expected to absorb shocks without access to monetary tools available to sovereign actors and without the exit options available to private capital. Bound by balanced-budget requirements and fixed obligations, municipalities become conduits through which macroeconomic risk is transmitted to neighborhoods.

Who Has the Power to Shed Risk

Risk moves toward those least able to refuse it.

Large financial institutions can diversify portfolios, hedge exposure, or exit markets altogether. Developers can restructure financing, delay construction, or abandon

---

[1] Elaine Draper, review of Risk, Society, and Social Theory, by Ulrich Beck, Mark Ritter, and Mary Douglas, Contemporary Sociology 22, no. 5 (1993): 641–44, https://doi.org/10.2307/2074588
.

projects when conditions shift. Capital can relocate across cities, regions, and asset classes in search of safer returns.

Residents cannot.

Households experience risk not as an abstract variable but as rent increases, tax reassessments, job precarity, service reductions, and displacement. These outcomes are often described as market effects or unintended consequences, but they are better understood as the final stage of risk transfer— when volatility engineered elsewhere settles into daily life. Risk does not disappear; it is lived.[2]

The question, then, is not whether risk exists, but who has the authority to pass it along and who is required to absorb it without consent.

Financial Instruments as Risk Conveyors

Urban development relies on tools that appear neutral but function as conduits. Municipal bonds defer present costs into the future, committing public revenue to long-term repayment. Tax increment financing pledges future tax receipts to stabilize current private investment, prioritizing present feasibility over future fiscal flexibility. Subsidized credit lowers borrowing costs while preserving market discipline downstream, ensuring that risk remains legible to investors even as it is softened by public support.[3]

---

[2] Timothy W. Morrissey, Yujin Cha, Shannon Wolf, and Munira Khan, "Household Economic Instability: Constructs, Measurement, and Implications," *Child & Youth Services* Review 118 (November 2020): 105502, https://doi.org/10.1016/j.childyouth.2020.105502

[3] James Sarra and Catherine L. Wade, "*Predatory Lending Practices Prior to the Global Financial Crisis,*" in *Predatory Lending and the Destruction of the African-American Dream* (Cambridge: Cambridge University Press, 2020), 23–68.

Each instrument shifts uncertainty forward in time and outward across institutions.

These tools are politically attractive because they obscure tradeoffs. Costs are delayed. Exposure is fragmented across budgets, agencies, and years. Responsibility is dispersed across technical instruments and institutional processes, rather than centralized in clearly visible or politically accountable decisions. By the time consequences materialize, they appear disconnected from original choices that set them in motion.

Risk has already moved.

Case Studies: When Risk Cannot Be Contained

Even when financing tools are presented as neutral instruments to spur development, multiple examples demonstrate that risk is not eliminated — it simply surfaces elsewhere.

St. Louis Mills Mall: Public Exposure, Private Gain and Regional Risk Transfer

The St. Louis Outlet Mall, formerly the St. Louis Mills Mall, offers a vivid illustration of how large-scale urban and suburban projects concentrate risk in public hands while stabilizing private expectations. Completed in 2003 at a cost of $250 million, the mall ultimately sold for just $4.4 million—a fraction of its original investment.[4] Yet the public exposure extended far beyond the mall itself, rooted in both municipal financing mechanisms and state-

---

[4] Alex Ihnen, "St. Louis Outlet Mall Sells for 98% Off," *NextSTL*, February 2016, https://nextstl.com/2016/02/st-louis-outlet-mall-sells-98-off/

backed infrastructure projects that enabled its development.[5]

The mall's construction was closely tied to transportation investments: Missouri Route 370, completed in 1996 at a cost of $250 million, and the Discovery Bridge were promoted as exemplary infrastructure projects, designed to relieve congestion on I-70 and stimulate economic growth in St. Charles County. Indeed, local media hailed MO-370 as "one of the more successful infrastructure projects ever undertaken in St. Charles County," citing the Mills Mall as the highway corridor's largest economic development benefit.[6] But the reality reveals a more complex pattern of risk transfer. Traffic data indicate that while MO-370 carried 55,000 vehicles daily by 2013, I-70 still handled 155,000 vehicles per day—showing that the highway primarily facilitated suburban expansion and induced demand rather than relieving congestion.[7]

These projects illustrate how public investment in infrastructure can serve private and regional economic objectives while leaving legacy liabilities for municipalities where growth failed to materialize. St. Louis County experienced population loss and stagnating job growth, even as St. Charles County prospered.[8] State and federal funds effectively subsidized sprawl, shifting both the benefits and risks of development across geographies. Cities like St. Louis became repositories of risk, absorbing the consequences of abandoned properties, declining retail

---

5 Ihnen, "St. Louis Outlet Mall Sells for 98% Off."
6 *Ibid.*
7 *Ibid.*
8 *Ibid.*

tax bases, and underutilized infrastructure, while the financial upside of growth accrued elsewhere.

The Mills Mall itself catalyzed a regional chain reaction. Nearby retail properties—including Northwest Plaza, Jamestown Mall, and Northland Plaza—closed as suburban investment concentrated in the new development.[9] Redevelopment efforts at these sites relied heavily on public subsidies, including Tax Increment Financing (TIF) and state tax credits, committing municipalities to long-term obligations while leaving residents and neighborhoods vulnerable to displacement and declining services. Even the Northwest Plaza, which sold for $5 million after closing, now benefits from a $106 million redevelopment subsidized by more than $40 million in public financing— a stark illustration of how risk is shifted onto public budgets while private actors retain upside potential.[10]

This regional pattern mirrors the chapter's central argument: risk is never eliminated—it is relocated across institutions, geographies, and social boundaries. In the St. Louis case, financial and infrastructure decisions created stability for investors and suburban municipalities while leaving urban residents, adjacent communities, and local governments to absorb volatility. The Mills Mall and its associated infrastructure exemplify the structural dynamics of modern development: publicly funded projects may appear neutral and beneficial, but they often externalize both financial and social risk, producing spatially concentrated instability in neighborhoods least equipped to absorb it.

---

[9] *Ibid.*
[10] *Ibid.*

The Kansas City Power & Light District: Public Risk, Private Vibrancy

The Power & Light District in downtown Kansas City provides a striking example of risk relocation in urban development. Despite high-profile crowds during major sporting events, including the Royals' 2014 World Series run, taxpayers remain on the hook for millions in subsidies for decades to come.

When the city issued \$295 million in bonds in 2006 to support the seven-block entertainment district developed by Cordish Co., two-thirds of the funding went toward site acquisition, parking garages, and public infrastructure such as streets and sewers.[11] Consulting projections at the time estimated that new city and state tax revenues generated by the district would fully cover annual debt service.[12] In reality, revenues ranged from \$4.5 million to \$5.4 million annually—only 25–30 percent of the roughly \$19.6 million debt service in fiscal year 2014.[13] The city's residents covered the remaining \$14.9 million from general funds, money that might otherwise have supported police, fire, and public services.[14] Refinancing lowered payments in the short term but extended obligations through 2040.[15]

Despite these financial burdens, the district has seen rising occupancy, increasing sales, and expanding residential

---

[11] Lynn Horsley, "Despite Large Power & Light District Crowds, Taxpayers Are Still on the Hook," *The Kansas City Star*, February 7, 2015, https://www.kansascity.com/news/politics-government/article9530081.html#storylink=cpy

[12] Horsley, "Despite Large Power & Light District Crowds."

[13] *Ibid.*

[14] *Ibid.*

[15] *Ibid.*

development. Executive director Nick Benjamin emphasizes non-financial benefits: downtown revitalization, national media exposure, and a generational "experience" for residents during events. These outcomes are real, visible, and culturally significant—but they do not mitigate the financial exposure borne by the public.

The Kansas City case mirrors patterns observed in other U.S. cities. The district's vibrancy and perceived success conceal the underlying risk transfer: private actors capture upside through property development, retail, and entertainment revenues, while public institutions absorb downside through debt guarantees and fiscal backstops. Residents may enjoy the district's amenities, yet they remain structurally insulated from the financial consequences. As in St. Louis and Chicago, urban development here demonstrates the persistent relocation of risk from investors to municipal budgets—and, indirectly, to the broader public.

Allentown, Pennsylvania: The Neighborhood Improvement Zone and Concentrated Risk

Allentown's Neighborhood Improvement Zone (NIZ) offers a clear case of fiscal instruments stabilizing investor returns while shifting risk to the public sector and residents. Established to attract developers and revitalize the downtown commercial corridor, the NIZ channeled hundreds of millions in tax incentives into a narrowly defined geographic area. Despite this influx, adjacent neighborhoods saw little benefit: poverty remained persistently high, median home values declined, and wage growth lagged compared to control cities.

A detailed study of the first five years of NIZ activity found that converting owner-occupied housing into rental properties contributed to declining neighborhood stability. Owner-occupied units, which generate positive externalities including better maintenance, civic engagement, and neighborhood stewardship, were increasingly replaced by rental units that prioritized financial return over community investment. This transition coincided with a 6.2 percent decrease in median home value for owner-occupied houses from 2013 to 2017—nearly $8,000—while control cities saw negligible losses.[16]

Even within the NIZ, improvements were largely confined to the targeted tract (Lehigh County Census Tract 97.01), which saw rising median income and property values, as well as modest increases in homeownership.[17] Surrounding block groups experienced stagnant growth or decline, demonstrating that public investment successfully elevated investor returns without producing broader neighborhood spillovers. The study notes that benefits within the NIZ are likely driven in part by new, wealthier residents, rather than long-term inhabitants, highlighting the displacement and risk relocation embedded in such development strategies.[18]

Allentown's experience underscores a central point of contemporary urban finance: large-scale public subsidies and tax incentives may produce visible, high-profile development, but they do not inherently improve living conditions for residents or redistribute risk equitably. Fiscal

---

[16] Christopher Woods, *Allentown's Neighborhood Improvement Zone: Five Years of Failed Community and Economic Development* (Lehigh Preserve Institutional Repository, 2019), 37–43.
[17] Woods, *Allentown's Neighborhood Improvement Zone*, 38–40.
[18] *Ibid.*

instruments like the NIZ can stabilize capital and defer costs to the public sector, while local households absorb volatility through declining property values, reduced service capacity, and rising housing pressures.

Stability at the Top, Instability Below

Periods of apparent macroeconomic stability often coincide with intensified local volatility. Low interest rates fuel asset appreciation and encourage speculative development. Rising values are celebrated as growth, even as affordability erodes and exposure accumulates beneath the surface.

When conditions tighten—rates rise and liquidity contracts—the adjustment does not occur evenly. Capital retreats upward into safer assets and larger markets. Municipal budgets strain under fixed obligations and declining flexibility. Households, by contrast, face immediate pressure through higher rents, tax increases, job insecurity, and service reductions.[19]

Stability is preserved where it is politically and financially prioritized. Instability emerges where it is tolerated, absorbed by communities positioned as buffers rather than as beneficiaries of growth. As aforementioned in the previous chapter, in Chicago, TIF districts direct future property tax revenues toward subsidizing development in select neighborhoods. While these incentives support commercial and residential projects, they often concentrate

---

[19] Harvey Galper, Kim Rueben, Richard Auxier, and Amanda Eng, *Municipal Debt: What Does It Buy and Who Benefits?* (Washington, DC: Urban Institute, December 2014), https://www.urban.org/sites/default/files/publication/33631/109047-municipal-debt-what-does-it-buy-and-who-benefits-.pdf

.

fiscal and social exposure locally. For example, in Pilsen, residents have actively opposed TIF expansions, citing fears of rising rents, gentrification, and displacement. The city's general fund absorbs uncertainty when projections fail, but households bear the immediate costs of volatility. This underscores the asymmetry of stability: investors and capital enjoy predictable returns, while neighborhoods absorb the shocks.

The Household as Shock Absorber

In this system, households function as shock absorbers. They absorb volatility generated elsewhere—through rising housing costs, reduced public services, and forced mobility. Their stability is treated as elastic, their displacement as manageable, and their loss as an acceptable margin of adjustment.

This is not incidental. It reflects a development model that externalizes economic adjustment onto those with the least leverage and the fewest alternatives. Scholars of political economy have long observed that risk redistribution follows existing hierarchies of race, class, and power.[20] Urban development operationalizes this pattern dynamic spatially, concentrating exposure in places already marked by exclusion.

Neighborhoods, in effect, become buffers sites where systemic instability is contained, normalized, and lived.

Why the Pattern Repeats

---

[20] Jodi Melamed. "Racial Capitalism." Critical Ethnic Studies 1, no. 1 (2015): 76–85. https://doi.org/10.5749/jcritethnstud.1.1.0076.

The repetition of this cycle across cities is not evidence of failure; it is evidence of design.

So long as development is evaluated primarily through financial performance and growth metrics, risk will continue to flow downward, away from capital and toward households and neighborhoods with the least capacity to absorb loss. So long as public intervention is justified as necessary to attract private capital, public exposure will expand without corresponding authority, leverage, or control over outcomes.

The language may change—resilience, sustainability, equity—but the underlying mechanism remains unless risk allocation itself is confronted. Without that confrontation, new vocabularies merely rebrand old arrangements, and instability is reproduced under more progressive names.

Conclusion: Seeing the Movement

When risk is conceptualized as mobile rather than contained, several urban paradoxes come into focus: why periods of growth coincide with persistent insecurity, why public subsidies increase even amid austerity, and why development initiatives often produce distrust despite seemingly benign intentions.

Risk is never eliminated. It is moved quietly, deliberately, and predictably through financial systems that displace exposure across institutions and onto households least able to refuse it.

The next chapter turns to one of the most powerful engines of this movement: monetary policy. By tracing how interest rate decisions made far from any city reshape borrowing conditions, investment behavior, and development feasibility, the analysis moves from structural principle to macroeconomic force, showing how decisions at the highest levels of the financial system settle into everyday urban life.

CHAPTER 6: Displacement is a Financial Outcome, Not A Cultural One

Displacement is often framed as a cultural or social phenomenon. Media accounts describe "neighborhood change," "gentrification," or "urban renewal" as the inevitable result of shifting tastes, lifestyles, or values. Residents are blamed for resisting "progress," while long-standing institutions celebrate new investment. These explanations obscure the true driver: finance. Displacement is not a consequence of cultural failure; it is the predictable endpoint of a series of financial and institutional decisions.[1]

By the time a family receives a rent increase or eviction notice, the structures that made that outcome possible have already been in motion for years, often decades. Risk has flowed downward from banks, investors, and city governments to households who have no meaningful capacity to absorb it. Understanding displacement as a financial outcome requires tracing that movement from macroeconomic decisions to municipal policy to everyday lived experience.

The Chain of Financial Forces

Displacement begins in the corridors of power most residents never see. Consider a hypothetical development in a low-income neighborhood:

---

[1] Taylor, *Race for Profit.*

A private developer identifies an opportunity to build an apartment complex on city-owned land. To finance construction, the developer secures a combination of commercial bank loans and private equity. Municipal authorities, eager to attract investment and signal growth, offer a tax increment financing (TIF) arrangement that diverts future property tax revenue to help service the project's debt. The city may also invest public funds in infrastructure such as streets, utilities, parks— anticipating that the project will raise surrounding property values and expand the tax base.[2]

These mechanisms reduce the developer's exposure to loss. But the risk does not disappear; it moves. It is absorbed by residents living in and around the project area. Rent increases, property tax reassessments and service pressures become the mechanism through which this financial exposure is transferred. Families who have lived in the neighborhood for decades find themselves priced out, not because they failed to adapt, but because the cost of stabilizing investment has been shifted onto them.[3]

Even in projects labeled "affordable," the outcome can be similar. Affordability is often pegged to area median income (AMI) benchmarks that reflect regional earnings rather than residents' historical wages. A unit designed as "moderate-income" may remain unattainable for households who have anchored the neighborhood for generations. Displacement occurs not despite affordability policy, but through its

---

[2] David L. Prytherch, "Reimagining the Physical/Social Infrastructure of the American Street: Policy and Design for Mobility Justice and Conviviality," *Urban Geography* 43, no. 5 (2022): 688–712, https://doi.org/10.1080/02723638.2021.1960690

[3] Aalbers, *The Financialization of Housing*.

design—when financial metrics substitute for lived economic reality.[4]

Brooklyn and New York City: Gentrification, Health, and Unequal Development

In Brooklyn and greater New York City, the story of urban development is inseparable from the forces of financing and market-driven investment, forces that shape neighborhoods long before architects draw plans or zoning hearings convene. Between 2000 and 2017, certain neighborhoods underwent rapid transformation, classified by researchers as hypergentrifying, gentrifying, or not gentrifying.[5] Hypergentrifying areas—Williamsburg-Bushwick, Bedford-Stuyvesant–Crown Heights, and Greenpoint in Brooklyn—experienced rent increases of over 100 percent.[6] These neighborhoods were joined by similar surges in Manhattan, Queens, and the Bronx, revealing a pattern of intense, concentrated investment in historically disinvested communities.[7] Gentrifying neighborhoods saw more

---

[4] Rodrigo Fernandez, "Financialization and Housing: Between Globalization and Varieties of Capitalism," in *The Financialization of Housing: A Political Economy Approach*, by Manuel B. Aalbers (London: Routledge, 2016), 97–116, https://doi.org/10.4324/9781315668666

[5] Karen A. Alroy et al., "Can Changing Neighborhoods Influence Mental Health? An Ecological Analysis of Gentrification and Neighborhood-Level Serious Psychological Distress—New York City, 2002–2015," *Department of Public Health Scholarship and Creative Works*, Montclair State University, 2023, accessed February 20, 2026, 6 https://digitalcommons.montclair.edu/cgi/viewcontent.cgi?article=12 20&context=public-health-facpubs

[6] Alroy et al., "Can Changing Neighborhoods Influence Mental Health?", 1

[7] Alroy et al., "Can Changing Neighborhoods Influence Mental Health?", 6

moderate increases, while not-gentrifying neighborhoods largely remained stable.

These economic shifts were mirrored by striking demographic changes. Hypergentrifying New York City neighborhoods saw the White population grow by nearly 7 percent, while Black residents declined by 6.4 percent and Latino residents by 3.5 percent.[8] Young adults between 25 and 44 increased by over 3 percent, further reshaping the age profile of these communities.[9] In contrast, gentrifying neighborhoods experienced smaller or even reversed trends, with slight decreases in White and Black populations and a modest increase in Latino residents. These numbers reveal that hypergentrification produces not only economic upheaval but also a profound reconfiguration of the racial and generational landscape.

The consequences of these transformations are not only material but also psychological. Residents' mental health, as measured by serious psychological distress, diverged along racial lines. In hypergentrifying neighborhoods, White residents experienced significant reductions in distress, while Black and Latino residents saw little change, remaining at higher levels of stress.[10] These trends demonstrate that the benefits of urban redevelopment are distributed unevenly, favoring new, often White, arrivals while longstanding residents—especially Black and Latino communities—bear the hidden costs of social disruption.

---

[8] Alroy et al., "Can Changing Neighborhoods Influence Mental Health?", 9

[9] *Ibid.*

[10] Alroy et al., "Can Changing Neighborhoods Influence Mental Health?", 6

Displacement is a Financial Outcome, Not A Cultural One

Housing tenure data further illustrate this tension. In hypergentrifying neighborhoods, the majority of Black and Latino residents had lived in the same home for five years or longer, compared with a smaller share of White residents. Many original residents remained in place, experiencing rising rents, neighborhood cultural shifts, and the stress of watching familiar spaces transform around them. The burden of gentrification, therefore, extends beyond displacement; it manifests in the daily psychological and social strain imposed on communities whose roots run deep in these neighborhoods.

Brooklyn's experience demonstrates vividly that development is, above all, a financing decision. Investment flows follow profit, not equity, reshaping neighborhoods in ways that amplify racial and economic disparities. Market-driven redevelopment delivers improvements in amenities, safety, and housing stock, but the benefits are unevenly distributed, often privileging White residents while imposing social and psychological costs on Black and Latino communities. In this sense, Brooklyn serves as a microcosm for the broader argument of this chapter: development is never neutral. Every project, every influx of capital, every decision about financing redistributes not only wealth but stress, opportunity or lack of thereof.

Philadelphia: Opportunity Zones, TIFs, and the Financial Mechanics of Displacement

Philadelphia's experience reinforces the core argument of this chapter: displacement is not a random social phenomenon but a predictable outcome of financialized development policy. Federal Opportunity Zones and tax-related incentives have been deployed across numerous historically disinvested corridors particularly in areas such as North Broad Street, Point Breeze, Grays Ferry, Kensington, and Port Richmond which were selected precisely because they combined high poverty, low home values, and proximity to job centers.[11] These criteria made them attractive for tax-preferred investment but also poised them for accelerated market pressure once capital flowed in.

Philadelphia's designated Opportunity Zone tracts recorded substantially larger home value and rent increases between 2010 and 2017 compared with eligible but non-selected areas: median home values rose by roughly 25.6 % and median rents by 28.2 %, outpacing increases of 12.4 % and 19.2 % in comparable neighborhoods.[12] These trends illustrate how place-based tax incentives can amplify market forces in targeted communities, driving up the cost of living for long-term residents.

At the same time, research from the Federal Reserve Bank of Philadelphia shows that losses of low-cost rental housing have been especially acute in gentrifying neighborhoods. Between 2000 and 2014, Philadelphia's census tracts defined as gentrifying — including University City and the Graduate Hospital area — lost over 23,600 units with rents

---

[11] Jacob Adelman, "Philly's 'Opportunity Zone' Tracts Are Some of the City's Poorest, and Among Its Biggest Gentrifiers, Fed Finds," Philadelphia Inquirer, November 15, 2019, https://www.inquirer.com/real-estate/commercial/opportunity-zones-philadelphia-federal-reserve-gentrification-poverty-development-20191115.html

[12] Federal Reserve Bank of Philadelphia, *How Are Cities Leveraging Opportunity Zones for Community Development?*, Community Development Reports (Philadelphia: Federal Reserve Bank of Philadelphia, November 2019), 11, https://www.philadelphiafed.org/-/media/frbp/assets/community-development/reports/1119-opportunity-zones.pdf

under $750 per month, at nearly five times the rate seen in non-gentrifying areas.[13] This reduction of affordable stock leaves lower-income households with fewer housing options and greater vulnerability to displacement pressures.

Together, these patterns reveal how financial tools like Opportunity Zones and tax increment incentives do not operate neutrally. By making investment more profitable in areas with existing market momentum even when those areas were historically redlined, policymakers effectively amplify capital flows into neighborhoods where property values and rents are already rising. That influx, in turn, accelerates property turnover and pushes lower-income households outward, not because of cultural choices or demographic preferences but because the financial architecture surrounding development reshapes incentives, risk, and reward.

Interest Rates and the Macro Connection

The role of the Federal Reserve and broader monetary policy is rarely acknowledged in discussions of neighborhood change, yet it is central. Low interest rates make borrowing cheaper, encouraging developers and investors to pursue highly leveraged projects. Cities, too, take advantage of inexpensive debt to finance infrastructure refinance

---

[13] Federal Reserve Bank of Philadelphia, "Philadelphia Fed Research Measures Impact of Gentrification on Low-Cost Housing Stock," *Federal Reserve Bank of Philadelphia Community Development,* accessed February 20, 2026, https://www.philadelphiafed.org/community-development/housing-and-neighborhoods/philadelphia-fed-research-measures-impact-of-gentrification-on-low-cost-housing-stock

obligations, or subsidize development in the hope of accelerating growth.[14]

When interest rates rise, the carrying costs of debt increase, placing immediate pressure on property owners to maximize revenue. Landlords raise rents to service higher financing costs. Developers shift toward luxury conversions or higher-margin uses that can sustain elevated debt obligations. Municipal budgets, often structured around projected property tax growth and fixed debt obligations, strain under commitments made in a different financial environment. Households in affected neighborhoods are left to absorb the adjustment.

In other words, displacement is embedded in the rhythm of macroeconomic policy. It is transmitted through financial instruments and municipal practices and realized in the lives of ordinary residents. It is not an accident; it is the predictable outcome of a system designed to protect investors and manage municipal risk, often at the expense of community stability.

Historical and Racial Context

As explained in the first part of the book, this financialized pattern intersects with history and race. Decades of redlining, disinvestment, and discriminatory lending created neighborhoods systematically excluded from wealth accumulation.[15] These areas were denied mortgage credit,

---

[14] Blyth, *Austerity: The History of a Dangerous Idea.*

[15] Meizhu Lui, Barbara Robles, Betsy Leondar-Wright, Rose Brewer, and Rebecca Adamson, The Color of Wealth: The Story Behind the U.S. Racial Wealth Divide (New York: The New Press, 2006), 73–130.

insurance, and public investment, producing the very conditions later cited as evidence of risk.

When such neighborhoods attract new investment today, they are treated as "high risk," justifying the extensive de-risking mechanisms. Ironically, the public subsidies and guarantees designed to make projects feasible often reinforce displacement rather than prevent it. Neighborhoods once neglected are now overexposed to financial tools designed to protect capital rather than residents.

The financial outcomes of displacement cannot be separated from these historical dynamics. Structural inequities amplify the effects of risk transfer. Families historically denied access to credit are now positioned to absorb volatility generated by capital flows that they neither control nor benefit from.

Institutions, Incentives, and Misaligned Goals

Municipal agencies and housing authorities play a critical role in channeling investment, but their incentives are often misaligned with resident stability. Agencies are rewarded for leveraging public dollars to attract private capital, not for preserving affordability or continuity over time.

Housing agencies may prioritize the rapid absorption of federal funds, favoring projects that can meet capital and compliance requirements over those aligned with long-term community needs. City finance departments focus on balanced budgets and creditworthiness, often relying on rising property tax revenue that comes at the expense of long-term residents. Even well-intentioned tools, such as inclusionary zoning, tax credits, or mixed-income mandates can accelerate displacement when underlying financial structures remain unchanged.

The pattern is consistent: institutions designed to facilitate development become vehicles for displacement. Residents are treated as buffers for financial risk rather than as protected stakeholders.

Speculation and Rational Behavior

Speculation is often blamed on "outside investors" or framed as a moral failing. Yet it is a rational response to the structure of incentives. Private actors seek to maximize returns while minimizing exposure. When municipalities absorb downside risk through abatements, subsidies, infrastructure guarantees, or regulatory flexibility, the rational response is to capture upside through rents, appreciation and asset turnover.[16]

The behavior of investors and developers is not pathological; it is structured. Households who are displaced are not being targeted culturally; they are the residual layer of risk in a system designed to shield capital and preserve municipal balance sheets.

Neighborhood Consequences Beyond Housing

Displacement reshapes more than housing markets; it alters the social and economic fabric of neighborhoods:

- Schools lose long-term enrollment, disrupting educational planning and funding.
- Local businesses lose steady customers, undermining economic sustainability.

---

[16] Roy, Larner, and Peck, "Book Review Symposium," 275.

- Social networks fragment, eroding informal systems of care and support.

These consequences are often interpreted as social or cultural failures. In reality, they are secondary effects of financial engineering. The harm is human, but the cause is structural.

Conclusion: Understanding Displacement as Predictable

Recognizing displacement as a financial outcome reframes the problem from moral or cultural blame to structural accountability. It allows cities, housing agencies, and residents to ask different questions:

- Who bears risk at each stage of the development process?
- How can financial instruments be redesigned to protect households rather than expose them?
- Which policies stabilize communities without freezing development?

Once displacement is understood as structured rather than accidental, the path to solutions becomes clearer.

Part III: INSTITUTIONS, INCENTIVES, AND FAILURE

CHAPTER 7: The Logic of Urban Change

Urban change is not the organic product of neighborhood preference; it is the spatial expression of financial systems operating far beyond the communities they transform. Urban neighborhoods are shaped by a complex web of financial, institutional, and historical forces. Rising property values, redevelopment projects, demographic shifts, and displacement are not random outcomes; they are predictable results of a system linking federal monetary policy, municipal finance, redevelopment agencies, and private capital. By the time cranes appear on the skyline, the financial decisions that will reshape the neighborhood have already been made. Understanding this chain allows policymakers, housing agencies, and investors to anticipate effects, design interventions, and align urban growth with community stability rather than displacement.[1]

Urban Change as Structured Incentive

Urban transformation does not occur in a theoretical vacuum. Long before contemporary debates about gentrification and displacement, scholars of urban political economy identified the structural logic through which cities pursue growth. In Urban Fortunes, John Logan and Harvey Molotch argued that urban development is best understood through the "growth machine" framework, in which

---

[1] Keeanga-Yamahtta Taylor, "Let the Buyer Beware," in Race for Profit: How Banks and the Real Estate Industry Undermined Black Homeownership (Chapel Hill, NC: University of North Carolina Press, 2019; online edition, North Carolina Scholarship Online, January 21, 2021), https://doi.org/10.5149/northcarolina/9781469653662.003.000

coalitions of local government officials, real estate interests, and financial actors align around the shared objective of increasing land values.[2] Within this framework, rising property values are not incidental outcomes but central performance metrics of urban governance.

What the growth machine literature identified at the metropolitan scale, theories of racial capitalism extend historically and structurally. Building on the work of scholars such as Cedric Robinson, racial capitalism emphasizes that capital accumulation has never been spatially or socially neutral; it has consistently relied on differentiated exposure to risk and unequal access to credit, land, and state protection.[3] When these perspectives are read together, the contemporary pattern becomes clearer: financialized urban development does not simply produce uneven outcomes — it systematically channels investment toward spaces where risk can be publicly managed and returns privately captured.

From this vantage point, the patterns documented in Brooklyn, Philadelphia, Detroit, Los Angeles, and Jersey City appear less as isolated case studies and more as expressions of a coherent institutional logic. Municipal actors pursue creditworthiness and tax base expansion; investors pursue yield and asset appreciation; redevelopment agencies pursue project feasibility within bond market constraints. Displacement emerges at the intersection of

---

[2] Harvey Molotch, "The City as a Growth Machine: Toward a Political Economy of Place," *American Journal of Sociology* 82, no. 2 (September 1976): 309–32, https://web.ics.purdue.edu/~hoganr/SOC%20602/Spring%202014/Molotch%201976.pdf

[3] Cedric J. Robinson, Black Marxism: The Making of the Black Radical Tradition (London: Pluto Press, 2019).

these aligned incentives. It is not the breakdown of the system. It is evidence that the system is operating as structured.

Federal Monetary Policy and Urban Capital Costs

At the top this chain sits the Federal Reserve, whose monetary policy determines the cost of borrowing nationwide. Low interest rates reduce the cost of capital for cities and investors alike, making municipal bonds real estate development, and leveraged projects appear more financially feasible. When rates rise, borrowing costs increase, and projects must be recalibrated, delayed, or abandoned.

During the post-2008 recovery, historically low interest rates enabled cities such as Detroit enter municipal bond markets and finance redevelopment in Midtown and downtown. These conditions attracted private investment in luxury apartments, entertainment districts, and commercial space.[45]The availability of cheap capital shaped not only *whether* development occurred, but *what kind* of development appeared feasible.

Monetary policy also shapes investor expectations. Low-cost capital encourages large-scale urban real estate investment by compressing risk premiums and making

---

[4] Andre M. Perry and Hannah Stephens, "Investment without Displacement: How a Surge of Development Changed—and Didn't Change—One Detroit Neighborhood," Brookings Institution, January 24, 2024, https://www.brookings.edu/articles/investment-without-displacement-how-a-surge-of-development-changed-and-didnt-change-one-detroit-neighborhood/

[5] James L. Tatum III, "Detroit's Bankruptcy and Market Reentry," *Emory Bankruptcy Developments* Journal 37, no. 1 (2020): 65–85, https://scholarlycommons.law.emory.edu/ebdj/vol37/iss1/5

returns appear relatively secure. High rates, by contrast, redirect capital toward safer or more predictable assets, constraining municipal redevelopment strategies. In this sense, local development outcomes are partially determined by national monetary policy decisions far removed from any specific neighborhood.[6]

The Municipal Bond Market as a Development Engine

Municipal bonds act as the primary conduit between federal monetary policy and local development. Cities issue bonds to finance infrastructure, public housing, and redevelopment projects, often backed by property tax revenue or tax increment financing (TIF) districts. The yield, structure, and market reception of these bonds determine both the scale and character of development cities can pursue.

Chicago as mentioned in previous chapters illustrates this dynamic clearly. Bond financing enabled large-scale riverfront redevelopment, transit-oriented projects, and neighborhood revitalization initiatives that would have been impossible under constrained local budgets. Investor confidence in the city's creditworthiness expanded development capacity. Yet these same mechanisms incentivized projects promising high returns, often prioritizing luxury housing over long-term affordability.[7] In this sense, Chicago's redevelopment trajectory illustrates

---

[6] Aaron Klein and Alan Cui, "Quantitative Easing and Housing Inflation Post-COVID," *Brookings Institution*, October 8, 2025, https://www.brookings.edu/articles/quantitative-easing-and-housing-inflation-post-covid/

[7] City of Chicago, *Bond Rating Outlook Downgrade*, November 6, 2025, Chicago Office of the CFO, https://www.chicago.gov/content/dam/city/depts/COFA/BondRating/Bond%20Rating%20outlook%20downgrade_11062025.pdf

how bond-financed growth strategies operationalize the urban growth machine, translating credit market confidence directly into spatial restructuring.

Additionally, in Los Angeles, bond-financed projects such as the Staples Center redevelopment catalyzed extensive private investment. Public debt and tax incentives were used to attract institutional capital, shaping not only project viability but spatial impact. While these initiatives produced visible growth, they also intensified displacement pressures in adjacent low-income neighborhoods.[89]

Redevelopment Agencies: Mission within Constraints

Redevelopment agencies translate financial capacity into actionable projects. Their mandate is dual: stimulate economic growth while maintaining fiscal stability. Yet their choices are constrained by upstream financial realities— bond yields, interest rates, and investor expectations—over which they have limited control.

Baltimore's redevelopment agency attempted to balance public objectives with private capital imperatives through mixed-income projects and affordability commitments. Operating within the constraints of bond financing and TIF structures, the result was uneven: increased revenue and

---

[8] Urban Displacement Project, "Los Angeles – Gentrification and Displacement," Urban Displacement Project, accessed January 31, 2026, https://www.urbandisplacement.org/maps/los-angeles-gentrification-and-displacement/

[9] City of Los Angeles Department of City Planning, Project Determination Document, Case No. MTY1MDK0 (Los Angeles: City of Los Angeles Department of City Planning, 2025), https://planning.lacity.gov/pdiscaseinfo/document/MTY1MDk0/fe3b456d-e5a5-4f0e-9fa7-879f1ff43502/pdd

physical redevelopment alongside rising rents and resident displacement.[10]

Detroit's redevelopment authorities faced similar limitations in the 2010s. Federal and municipal incentives enabled large-scale downtown investment, but the financial architecture favored investor stability over community continuity. Displacement in historically African American neighborhoods followed predictable patterns, not policy failure.[11] This pattern reflects the growth-oriented logic identified in *Urban Fortunes*, where municipal policy and private capital align around land-value expansion even when neighborhood stability erodes.[12]

Private Capital and Market Responses

Private investors and developers respond rationally to the incentives embedded in federal and municipal finance. When public guarantees, subsidies and infrastructure investments reduce downside risk, maximizing returns becomes the expected behavior.

Jersey City's high-rise luxury developments boom reflects this logic. Zoning changes, public infrastructure investment,

---

[10] Brett Theodos, Eric Hangen, Brady Meixell, and Lionel Foster, *The East Baltimore Development Initiative: A Long-Term Impact Evaluation of a Comprehensive Community Initiative* (Washington, DC: Urban Institute, November 2022), 6, https://www.urban.org/sites/default/files/2022-10/The%20East%20Baltimore%20Development%20Initiative.pdf

[11] Steve Neavling, "Black Detroiters Are Fleeing the City at an Alarming Rate," Metro Times, March 29 – April 4, 2023, https://www.metrotimes.com/news/black-detroiters-are-fleeing-the-city-at-an-alarming-rate-32716634

[12] John R. Logan and Harvey L. Molotch, *Urban Fortunes: The Political Economy of Place*, 20th Anniversary ed. (Berkeley: University of California Press, 2007).

and affordable housing requirements created a development environment structured around capital attraction. Investor expectations shaped by bond financing ultimately determined project composition, resulting in rising housing costs and intensified pressure on long-term residents—not through negligence, but through design.[13]

For example, in Jersey City, the trajectory of contemporary urban development is neither accidental nor purely the outcome of market forces. Rather, it emerges from a deliberately structured set of municipal incentives, capital market logics, and fiscal imperatives that collectively favor large-scale, high-return projects. Central to this dynamic is the city's extensive use of long-term tax abatements and PILOT agreements (Payments in Lieu of Taxes)—distinct but complementary development incentives—which have become a defining feature of its high-rise luxury boom.[14] By the late 2010s, Jersey City maintained hundreds of active abatements, the majority concentrated along the Hudson waterfront in areas such as Paulus Hook, Newport, and Journal Square.[15][16] These agreements, often lasting two to

---

[13] Chris Fry, "New Report Details the Depths of Jersey City's Housing Shortage," Jersey Digs, December 17, 2024, https://www.jerseydigs.com/jersey-city-housing-shortage/

[14] Jonathan Wharton, *Abatement Addiction: A Case Study on Jersey City's Municipal Tax Abatements, Urban Gentrification and the Politics of Rights* (paper presented at the APSA 2011 Annual Meeting, 2011), SSRN, https://papers.ssrn.com/sol3/papers.cfm?abstract_id=1901269

[15] Wharton, *Abatement Addiction*.

[16] Chelsea Pujols, "As Rents Surge in Jersey City, Mayoral Candidates Offer Diverging Plans on Affordable Housing," *Jersey Vindicator*, July 22, 2025, https://jerseyvindicator.org/2025/07/22/as-rents-surge-in-jersey-city-mayoral-candidates-offer-diverging-plans-on-affordable-housing/

three decades, substantially reduced developers' tax burdens during the period when project returns were highest. While originally intended to stimulate investment in distressed neighborhoods, critics and city officials alike observed that these incentives were overwhelmingly captured by already desirable waterfront zones, signaling a recalibration of public policy to favor financeable, large-scale development over the stabilization of existing communities.[17]

Spatial patterns of growth further reflect the rationality of this system. Development has clustered in capital-intensive areas offering proximity to Manhattan, access to the PATH transit system, and parcels large enough to support dense, high-rise construction.[18] Zoning overlays and preexisting infrastructure amplified the financial feasibility of these projects, effectively channeling investment to zones where returns could be maximized. In this sense, the geography of Jersey City's development mirrors the imperatives of capital itself: projects materialize where financing is predictable, risks are mitigated, and profits scale efficiently. The resulting landscape is not a happenstance of demand, but the intended outcome of an incentive structure carefully calibrated to attract institutional investment.

Empirical indicators of this phenomenon are unmistakable in the city's housing market. During the luxury construction boom of the 2010s, median rents in waterfront high-rises routinely exceeded $3,000 per month for a one-bedroom

---

[17] Pujols, "As Rents Surge in Jersey City, Mayoral Candidates Offer Diverging Plans on Affordable Housing."

[18] JLL Secures $384 Million for Jersey City's Harborside 8 Luxury Waterfront Development," *Resident.com* press release, December 26, 2025, https://resident.com/press-releases/2025/12/26/jll-secures-384-million-for-jersey-citys-harborside-8-luxury-waterfront-development

unit, situating Jersey City among the most expensive rental markets in New Jersey.[19] Simultaneously, the stock of lower-cost housing stagnated or declined, generating pronounced displacement pressures in adjacent neighborhoods.[20] These outcomes were not anomalous but consistent with the financial logics underpinning municipal decision-making: reduced developer risk, favorable zoning, and long-term abatements combined to produce predictable rent escalation and spatial inequality.

Even the city's inclusionary zoning policies, which mandated a portion of units in certain developments be affordable, were implemented in ways that maintained project feasibility. Developers often received density bonuses, negotiated affordability terms, and abatements that preserved the financial attractiveness of their projects. This "feasibility-constrained inclusion" ensured that affordable housing obligations did not undermine the overarching objective of capital attraction. In practice, these policies functioned less as redistributive interventions and more as instruments for sustaining investor confidence while reproducing the upscale development trajectory. For example, in 2013 when the city's former Mayor Steven Fulop was elected as the city's Mayor, he introduced a tiered system of PILOT agreements which incentivized development in the "desirable" downtown section of the city inclusive of the Waterfront but also lesser desirable parts of the city such as Journal Square and the Bergen Lafayette sections and introduced inclusionary zoning variances where

---

[19] Pujols, "As Rents Surge in Jersey City, Mayoral Candidates Offer Diverging Plans on Affordable Housing."
[20] *Ibid.*

10%-15% of development units would be designated to affordable housing.[21]

Underlying these local incentives is a structural fiscal reality: Jersey City's municipal revenues increasingly depend on development-driven growth.[22] PILOT agreements, which channel payments directly to the city rather than entirely to school districts, created strong incentives for officials to favor high-value developments that expand the tax base.[23] Public officials frequently linked the city's fiscal health to the pace and scale of waterfront construction, embedding the pursuit of investor-oriented projects within the operational logic of municipal governance.[24] These initiatives aggrandized the development of the Downtown section of Jersey City while concomitantly causing "gentrification" throughout the City specifically in the Bergen Lafayette, Journal Square and the Heights sections of the city. In this environment, acting outside the financial system—resisting high-rise luxury construction or prioritizing community stability over ratable growth—would not merely be politically difficult; it would imperil the city's broader budgetary equilibrium.[25]

Finally, Jersey City's development boom cannot be fully understood without considering regional capital flows. The city functions as a secondary financialized housing market for Manhattan commuters, absorbing spillover demand generated by the high cost of New York City housing. This

---

[21] Benjamin Schneider, "Learning from Jersey City," *Vital City*, September 17, 2025, https://www.vitalcitynyc.org/articles/learning-from-jersey-city

[22] Schneider, "Learning from Jersey City."

[23] *Ibid.*

[24] *Ibid.*

[25] *Ibid.*

interconnection underscores that local development outcomes are inextricably tied to broader capital markets: Jersey City's skyline expansion is shaped not solely by municipal policy, but by regional financial dynamics that condition investor expectations and constrain the choices available to city officials.

Taken together, these factors illustrate a fundamental point: the composition and location of Jersey City's luxury developments are not accidental, nor are they simply responsive to consumer demand. They are strongly structured and constrained outcomes arising from municipal finance tools, zoning frameworks, fiscal dependence, and the gravitational pull of regional capital markets. The city's experience confirms that urban change—like that observed in Brooklyn or Philadelphia—is predictable when analyzed through the lens of financialized development, in which incentives, not oversight failures or resident choices, determine the form, pace, and social consequences of investment.

Jersey City's experience underscores that contemporary urban luxury development is less a market accident than the expected outcome of incentive structures embedded in municipal finance and capital markets.

Historical Inequities and Neighborhood Vulnerability

Financialized development interacts with historical inequities. Neighborhoods subjected to redlining, segregation, and long-term disinvestment carry structural vulnerabilities that amplify redevelopment pressure.

In Philadelphia as previously mentioned, long-neglected neighborhoods targeted for revitalization proved particularly exposed. Residents' limited access to credit and accumulated wealth reduced their ability to absorb rising costs, increasing displacement risk once investment arrived.[26] Historically produced vulnerability and modern financial engineering converge, demonstrating how racialized spatial inequality becomes an input into, rather than a byproduct of, urban investment strategy.

In Los Angeles, historically redlined neighborhoods such as South Central and Boyle Heights experienced similar dynamics. Once bond-financed projects and institutional capital entered, historical exclusion translated directly into vulnerability. Financialized development did not correct inequality; it activated it.[27] Across these cases, a consistent transmission mechanism becomes visible. Monetary policy shapes the price of capital; bond markets translate that price into municipal fiscal capacity; local governments deploy incentives to attract investment; and private developers respond by pursuing projects that maximize protected returns. What appears on the ground as neighborhood change is therefore the downstream expression of decisions made far upstream. By the time displacement pressures materialize in rents, property tax assessments, or land turnover, the underlying financial architecture has already structured the outcome. Urban change, in this sense, is not episodic or accidental—it is the predictable spatial footprint of a system that prioritizes capital stability over residential continuity. What appears locally as neighborhood change is, at the system level, the predictable spatial expression of

---

[26] Lei Ding, Jackelyn Hwang, and Eileen Divringi, "Gentrification and Residential Mobility in Philadelphia," *Regional Science and Urban Economics* 61 (September 2016): 38–51, https://doi.org/10.1016/j.regsciurbeco.2016.09.004

[27] City of Los Angeles Department of City Planning, Project Determination Document (Case No. MTY1MDK0), 2025.

capital seeking protected yield within publicly de-risked environments.

Predictable Outcomes of Financialized Urban Development

The combined effects of monetary policy, municipal finance, redevelopment agencies, and private capital produce outcomes that are remarkably consistent. Rising rents, demographic turnover, and displacement are systemic rather than accidental. Schools, small businesses, and social networks experience secondary disruptions, financial decisions made far upstream cascade downward.

Understanding these dynamics allows policymakers, agencies, and investors to anticipate outcomes rather than react to crises after displacement has occurred.

Toward Strategic Alignment

Recognizing the financial and institutional chain connecting the Federal Reserve to neighborhoods enables cities to act proactively. Bond structures can be designed to support affordability. Redevelopment agencies can be empowered to mediate market pressure rather than merely facilitate it. Financial guarantees can balance investor security with resident stability.

The logic of urban change is neither mysterious nor inevitable. It is a predictable system shaped by monetary policy, capital markets, institutional incentives, and historical legacies. Once understood, it becomes governable. Cities that confront this chain directly can align growth with stability, investment with trust, and development with long-term inclusion.

The language of municipal "choice" must be read within the architecture of constraint that governs contemporary urban finance. Cities—particularly those with large Black populations and Black political leadership—do not operate on an open policy field. Access to private capital, bond ratings, and federal development incentives conditions what is politically legible and fiscally permissible. Projects that align with investor expectations are rewarded with liquidity and favorable underwriting, while alternative development pathways risk credit downgrades, capital flight, or the withdrawal of federal support. In this environment, market-conforming redevelopment appears less as a freely chosen strategy than as the narrow corridor within which municipal officials are permitted to act. The result is a system in which local governments formally authorize urban change but do so under the disciplining pressure of financial markets and federal policy design. Hence, urban change, in other words, is not something cities simply experience, it is something they structure, finance, and ultimately choose.

CHAPTER 8: Housing Agencies Between Mission and Markets

Housing agencies occupy one of the most precarious positions in the urban political economy. They are tasked with delivering affordability, stability, and equity while operating within financial systems designed to reward efficiency, revenue generation, and risk minimization. This tension is not accidental. It is structural. Housing agencies are expected to solve problems produced upstream by monetary policy, capital markets, and municipal finance using tools that are themselves shaped by those same forces.[1]

Understanding housing agencies therefore requires moving beyond caricatures of bureaucratic failure or political inertia. Their decisions reflect continuous negotiation between mission and markets, public accountability and financial viability, resident stability and investor confidence.

The Institutional Mission of Housing Agencies

Public housing authorities, housing departments, and redevelopment-linked housing agencies are formally guided by social mandates: expand affordable housing, prevent displacement, improve habitability, and ensure fair access. These mandates are encoded in enabling legislation, federal

---

[1] Norbert J. Michel, *Strict Bank-Like Capital Rules Needed for Fannie Mae and Freddie Mac*, Backgrounder No. 3474 (Washington, DC: The Heritage Foundation, March 9, 2020), https://www.heritage.org/sites/default/files/2020-03/BG3474.pdf

housing programs, HUD regulations, and municipal policy frameworks.[2]

Yet housing agencies are not purely regulatory bodies. They are also asset managers. They own and dispose of land, manage portfolios, issue requests for proposals, structure public–private partnerships, and underwrite complex development deals. Their performance is increasingly evaluated not only through social outcomes but through balance sheets, compliance metrics, delivery timelines, and credit exposure.

This dual identity places housing agencies in a structurally conflicted position.

In cities such as Baltimore and Philadelphia, agencies are expected to stabilize distressed neighborhoods while simultaneously catalyzing private investment. The mission is expansive; the resources are constrained. The resulting gap between responsibility and capacity forces agencies to prioritize projects that are financially executable rather than socially optimal, projects that can close rather than those that best meet long-term community needs.[34]

---

[2] Yonah Freemark, Mel Langness, Amanda Hermans, Gabe Samuels, Tomi Rajninger, and David Blount, *Is Federal Infrastructure Investment Advancing Equity Goals?* (Washington, DC: Urban Institute, October 2023), 6, https://www.urban.org/sites/default/files/2023-10/Is%20Federal%20Infrastructure%20Investment%20Advancing%20Equity%20Goals.pdf

[3] Theodos et al., *Neighborhood Investment Flows in Baltimore*.

[4] Econsult Corporation, Penn Institute for Urban Research, and May 8 Consulting, Vacant Land Management in Philadelphia: The Costs of the Current System and the Benefits of Reform (Philadelphia: Penn Institute for Urban Research, March 17, 2010), https://www.urban.org/sites/default/files/publication/102976/neighborhood-investment-flows-in-baltimore_1.pdf

Funding Constraints and Financial Dependency

Housing agencies do not operate with fiscal sovereignty. Their budgets are structured by federal appropriations, municipal transfers, bond covenants, and the volatility of tax-credit markets. They function within financial constraints defined elsewhere.

Over time, direct federal funding for public housing has declined, replaced by competitive grants, public–private partnerships, and debt-financed redevelopment.[5] What was once funded through stable appropriations is now assembled through layered financing mechanisms that require alignment with investor expectations, underwriting standards, and repayment schedules.

Programs such as LIHTC, HOME funds, and Section 8 vouchers have become indispensable, but each carries binding constraints. LIHTC projects must satisfy investor underwriting standards and return expectations. Housing vouchers depend on private landlords' willingness to participate. Bond-financed developments require stable revenue streams over long horizons. These dependencies reshape agency behavior, pushing decisions toward financial viability rather than durability of affordability.

As seen in Jersey City, housing agencies increasingly rely on inclusionary zoning and negotiated affordability rather than direct public housing production. The result is affordability that exists on paper but remains bounded by compliance

---

[5] Center on Budget and Policy Priorities, *Public Housing*, Policy Basics (Washington, DC: Center on Budget and Policy Priorities, updated September 30, 2024), https://www.cbpp.org/research/housing/public-housing

periods, market conditions, and enforcement capacity rather than permanent public stewardship.[6]

Risk Management as a Governing Logic

As housing agencies have become more financially exposed, risk management has quietly displaced social need as the dominant governing logic. Projects are evaluated not only for community impact, but for execution risk, political risk, and financial risk.

High-need neighborhoods are often classified as high-risk, characterized by weaker market comparables, complex land assembly processes, heightened political scrutiny, and residents with limited access to credit. As a result, agencies frequently favor mixed-income or market-adjacent projects that appear safer to lenders and bondholders, even when unmet need is greatest elsewhere.[7]

Detroit's post-bankruptcy housing strategy illustrates this dynamic. Despite explicit equity goals, redevelopment clustered in areas with existing market momentum and stronger revenue prospects. Deeply distressed neighborhoods received fewer resources—not necessarily because of indifference, but because the prevailing financial

---

[6] City of Jersey City, *Mayor Introduces Inclusionary Zoning Ordinance*, press release, November 19, 2021, https://www.jerseycitynj.gov/news/pressreleases2021/mayor_introduces_inclusionary_zoning_ordinance

[7] Daniel Hornung, *States Can Ensure New Low-Income Housing Resources Get More Affordable Housing Built* (Washington, DC: Urban Institute, July 2025), https://www.urban.org/sites/default/files/2025-07/States_Can_Ensure_New_Low-Income_Housing_Resources_Get_More_Affordable_Housing_Built.pdf
.

architecture made them more difficult to underwrite and less attractive to capital.

Within the logic of the system, these decisions were rational. Underwriting standards prioritized predictability, revenue stability, and risk mitigation. Yet the spatial consequences were profound. Investment followed strength, while vulnerability compounded in the areas left behind.[8]

The Political Economy of "Feasibility"

"Feasibility" has become the most powerful word in housing policy discourse. It functions as a neutral-sounding proxy for market acceptability.

Projects deemed infeasible rarely fail because they lack social merit. They fail because they cannot be reconciled with financing structures, investor return thresholds, or municipal credit constraints. Housing agencies internalize these limits. Over time, staff and leadership adapt expectations, proposing what can pass underwriting rather than what communities most need.

The result is incrementalism: modest affordability set-asides, time-limited covenants, pilot programs, and partial mitigation measures that avoid systemic change.[9]

---

[8] Sugrue, "The Damning Mark of False Prosperities," 130.

[9] City of Los Angeles Department of City Planning, Chapter 2: *Constraints on Housing Maintenance, Improvement, and Development,* in Housing Element 2021–2029 (Los Angeles: City of Los Angeles Department of City Planning, 2025), https://planning.lacity.gov/odocument/321ad572-c89a-4759-9b4b-b4e7e29769a7/Chapter_2_-_Constraints_on_Housing_Maintenance_and_Development.pdf

In Los Angeles, for example, housing production has increased in numerical terms, yet affordability has grown progressively shallower relative to income. Units are delivered, but long-term accessibility remains fragile. The system rewards unit counts over stability, compliance over structural change, and speed over permanence.[10]

Accountability Without Power

Housing agencies are among the most scrutinized public institutions, yet they often possess the least discretionary power. They are accountable upward to federal regulators, sideways to municipal governments, outward to communities, and financially to lenders and investors. These accountabilities frequently conflict.

When displacement occurs, agencies face public backlash despite lacking authority over interest rates, land values, or speculative investment flows. The result is a legitimacy crisis: residents perceive agencies as complicit, while agencies experience themselves as constrained intermediaries.[11]

This contradiction is especially visible in historically Black neighborhoods, where agencies are charged with stabilization while operating in a capital environment that

---

[10] City of Los Angeles Department of City Planning, *Chapter 2: Constraints on Housing Maintenance, Improvement, and Development.*
[11] Miriam Zuk, Ariel H. Bierbaum, Karen Chapple, Karolina Górska, and Anastasia Loukaitou-Sideris, "Gentrification, Displacement, and the Role of Public Investment," *Journal of Planning Literature* 33, no. 1 (2017): 31–44, https://doi.org/10.1177/0885412217716439

rewards land value appreciation. The tension is structural, not personal.[12]

Housing Agencies as Shock Absorbers

Housing agencies function less as architects of urban change and more as shock absorbers for market volatility. When capital floods into cities, agencies are expected to soften displacement. When capital retreats, they are expected to maintain production with fewer resources. This asymmetry ensures that agencies are perpetually reactive.

The system relies on housing agencies to mitigate harm without altering its sources. Even well-designed policies struggle to counter upstream financial pressures. Without structural reform, agencies are confined to managing outcomes rather than shaping trajectories.

Reframing the Role of Housing Agencies

A sustainable urban housing strategy requires redefining what housing agencies are empowered to do. This includes longer affordability horizons, expanded public land stewardship, alternative financing structures, and insulation from short-term market volatility.

Cities that treat housing agencies as transactional deal managers limit their capacity to deliver stability. By contrast, agencies positioned as long-term steward— rather than facilitators of capital— can align public mission with durable outcomes. Achieving this shift requires political

---

[12] Jamila Michener, ed., *Poverty & Race*, vol. 32, no. 1 (January–March 2023), *Poverty & Race Research Action* Council, Washington, DC, 2023, 1–24, https://www.prrac.org/newsletters/Jan-March2023.pdf

will, fiscal innovation, and a willingness to challenge prevailing market logics.[13]

Housing agencies are not failing their missions. They are operating exactly as the system allows. Understanding this reality is a prerequisite for reform that moves beyond rhetoric toward structural change.

---

[13] Mark L. Joseph, "Is Mixed-Income Development an Antidote to Urban Poverty?" *Housing Policy Debate* 17, no. 2 (2006): 209–234, https://case.edu/socialwork/np3-nurturing-communities/sites/default/files/2018-09/Joseph-2006-Is-Mixed-Income-Development-an-Antidote-to-Urban-Poverty.pdf

CHAPTER 9: Investors, Impact, and the Limits of ESG

Over the past decade, investors have increasingly positioned themselves as partners in urban equity. Environmental, Social, and Governance (ESG) frameworks promise a reconciliation between profit and public purpose, offering cities and housing agencies a vocabulary through which private capital can be mobilized in the name of social good. The premise is compelling: align returns with responsibility, and markets will deliver equity.

Yet despite its rhetorical appeal, ESG has proven limited in its ability to alter the underlying dynamics of urban development. Capital still demands predictable returns. Underwriting standards still privilege revenue stability over long-term affordability. Projects must still satisfy financial thresholds before they satisfy social goals.

The persistent gap between intent and outcome reflects not moral failure, but systemic constraint.[1] ESG operates within a system designed to price risk, protect investment, and preserve liquidity. Without altering that architecture, it can moderate outcomes at the margins—but it cannot fundamentally reorganize the distribution of risk, reward, and power that shapes urban space.

Why Capital Turned to ESG

---

[1] Competitive Enterprise Institute, *Environmental, Social, and Governance Theory* (Washington, DC: Competitive Enterprise Institute, 2025), https://www.cei.org/studies/environmental-social-and-governance-theory/

The rise of ESG investing reflects both reputational and financial incentives. Institutional investors face growing pressure from regulators, pension beneficiaries, and the public to demonstrate social responsibility. ESG frameworks respond to this pressure by offering standardized metrics that can be incorporated into existing risk management and reporting systems without fundamentally altering investment strategy.[2]

In urban real estate, ESG allows investors to frame redevelopment projects as socially beneficial while preserving established return thresholds. Energy-efficient buildings, mixed-income housing components, and community benefit agreements function as visible indicators of impact. Yet these measures often assess inputs and processes rather than long-term outcomes, enabling alignment without transformation.

Cities across the United States— including New York City, Chicago and Los Angeles— have actively courted ESG-aligned investors, presenting redevelopment as both financially sound and socially responsible. This alignment

---

[2] Pedro Matos, ESG and Responsible Institutional Investing Around the World: A Critical Review (Washington, DC: CFA Institute Research Foundation, May 2020), 49–56, https://www.cfainstitute.org/sites/default/files/-/media/documents/book/rf-lit-review/2020/rflr-esg-and-responsible-institutional-investing.pdf

has unlocked capital flows, but it has not materially altered affordability trajectories or displacement dynamics.[34]

The Financial Logic ESG Cannot Escape

ESG operates within the same financial logic as conventional investment. Capital remains mobile, returns remain benchmarked, and risk remains priced. ESG screens may exclude certain assets or discourage particular practices, but they do not redefine profitability itself or displace the primacy of return.

In practice, ESG-aligned urban investments tend to cluster around projects that are already market-viable. Deep affordability, long-term rent stabilization, and non-extractive ownership models often fall outside acceptable risk thresholds. Investors may accept modestly reduced returns, in exchange for reputational or regulatory benefits, but they rarely tolerate prolonged uncertainty, structural illiquidity, or exposure that cannot be hedged or securitized.[5]

Jersey City's luxury towers with affordable set-asides illustrate this logic. Projects satisfy ESG criteria through

---

[3] City of New York Office of Management and Budget, Fiscal Year 2026–2035 Ten-Year Capital Strategy (New York, NY: City of New York Office of Management and Budget, 2025), https://www.nyc.gov/assets/omb/downloads/pdf/exec25/typ5-25.pdf

[4] Steven Cohen, "A Quarter of the 21st Century Over: What We've Learned about Sustainability and What Might Be Next," *Columbia University School of Professional Studies*, December 29, 2025, https://sps.columbia.edu/news/quarter-21st-century-over-what-weve-learned-about-sustainability-and-what-might-be-next

[5] Cong Zhang, Umar Farooq, Dima Jamali, and Mohammad Mahtab Alam, "The Role of ESG Performance in the Nexus between Economic Policy Uncertainty and Corporate Investment," *Research in International Business and Finance* 70, Part B (June 2024): 102358, https://doi.org/10.1016/j.ribaf.2024.102358

inclusionary units and energy standards, yet still contribute to neighborhood-wide rent escalation. The social benefit is partial, spatially limited, and time-bound.[6]

Impact Measurement Versus Lived Outcomes

A central limitation of ESG lies in measurement. ESG metrics privilege what can be quantified: units produced, emissions reduced, capital deployed. Outcomes that matter most to residents—displacement avoided, community continuity preserved, intergenerational stability sustained—are far harder to measure and therefore easier to exclude.

In Baltimore, ESG-aligned redevelopment projects reported compliance with affordability benchmarks even as surrounding neighborhoods experienced rising property taxes and indirect displacement. Metrics captured the project footprint but ignored spatial spillovers and temporal effects.[7]

This gap allows investors to claim success while communities experience loss. The issue is not insincerity, but the misalignment between financial reporting frameworks and social reality.

The Asymmetry of Risk and Reward

Urban redevelopment distributes risk asymmetrically. Investors face financial risk—quantified, diversified, and

---

[6] State of New Jersey Department of Community Affairs, *State of New Jersey Annual Action Plan 2023* (Trenton, NJ: New Jersey Department of Community Affairs, Division of Housing and Community Resources, 2023), https://www.nj.gov/dca/dhcr/links/State_of_NJ_AAP_2023.pdf

[7] Maryland Department of Housing and Community Development, "ReBUILD Metro: 'Reinvest Baltimore Is a Complete Game Changer,'" press release, July 30, 2025, https://news.maryland.gov/dhcd/2025/07/30/reinvest-baltimore-spotlight-rebuild-metro/

often hedged or insured. Residents face existential risk: displacement, housing insecurity, community fragmentation, and the erosion of social networks. ESG frameworks, for all their emphasis on measurable impact, rarely account for this fundamental imbalance.

When projects underperform, investors can restructure, refinance, or exit. Residents cannot. They remain in neighborhoods reshaped by rising costs, reduced stability, and diminished access. This structural imbalance explains why ESG, despite its good intentions, often reproduces inequality rather than mitigating it. Without institutional mechanisms designed to absorb and stabilize resident risk, impact remains procedural—measured in disclosures and compliance metrics—rather than transformative in lived experience.[8]

Detroit's post-crisis redevelopment highlights this point. Capital concentrated in stabilized districts delivered returns and visible revitalization, while residents in adjacent neighborhoods absorbed rising costs without commensurate protections.[9]

Public De-Risking and Private Upside

Most ESG-aligned urban investments depend on extensive public de-risking: tax abatements, subsidies, zoning concessions, and infrastructure investments. These

---

[8] Danielle Preziuso and Philip Odonkor, "Governance Gaps in Urban Decarbonization: Illuminating Structural Exclusion in Residential Energy Transitions," *Energy & Environmental Sustainability* 1, no. 4 (December 2025): 100054, https://doi.org/10.1016/j.eesus.2025.100054
[9] Perry and Stephens, "Investment without Displacement."

interventions reduce uncertainty and enhance returns, yet the upside remains privately captured.

Housing agencies and cities often justify these arrangements as necessary to attract capital. But the trade-off is rarely symmetrical. Public value is front-loaded; private value compounds over time. ESG does not challenge this structure. It legitimizes it.[10]

Los Angeles's transit-oriented developments exemplify this pattern. Significant public investment enabled ESG-branded projects, but long-term affordability protections remained limited relative to the scale of public support.

When ESG Becomes a Constraint on Policy

Paradoxically, ESG can narrow public ambition. Cities increasingly design projects to meet investor expectations rather than community needs, constraining policy imagination. Housing agencies, already operating under financial pressure, internalize ESG metrics as proxies for success.

This dynamic reinforces a recurring theme: institutions manage feasibility rather than outcomes. ESG becomes an additional compliance layer—another reporting framework—rather than a vehicle for structural change.

Beyond ESG: Toward Structural Alignment

The limitations of ESG do not imply that private capital has no role in equitable development. They underscore the need for structural alignment. This includes longer affordability

---

[10] Steffen Wetzstein, "The Global Urban Housing Affordability Crisis," *Urban Studies* 54, no. 14 (2017): 3159–77, https://doi.org/10.1177/0042098017711649

horizons, shared-equity models, public land stewardship, and financing mechanisms that price social risk alongside financial risk.

Meaningful impact requires changing the rules of participation, not merely improving disclosure. Investors can contribute, but only within frameworks that redefine success beyond short- and medium-term returns.

Cities that pursue these models move from impact branding to institutional design. The result is not anti-market, but post-ESG: a system that treats markets as tools rather than arbiters of urban value.

The Credibility Gap

The future of ESG in urban development depends on credibility. Communities increasingly distinguish between symbolic inclusion and material protection. Investors who fail to engage this reality face reputational backlash and political resistance.

For cities, the challenge is not whether to engage private capital, but how. ESG is a starting point, not a solution. Without structural reform, the promise of impact investing will remain constrained by the very markets it seeks to humanize.

Part IV: WHAT SUSTAINABLE DEVELOPMENT ACTUALLY REQUIRE

CHAPTER 10: What Accountability Looks Like in Practice?

Accountability has become one of the most frequently invoked and least clearly defined terms in urban development discourse. Cities promise accountability to residents. Investors demand accountability from public partners. Housing agencies are audited for compliance. ESG frameworks claim to operationalize accountability through metrics and disclosures. Yet despite this proliferation of accountability language, urban outcomes remain strikingly consistent: displacement, erosion of affordability, and the concentration of gains alongside the diffusion of costs.[1]

The persistence of these outcomes suggests that accountability, as currently practiced, is misaligned with power. It is measured where authority is weakest and deferred where decision-making influence is greatest. To understand what accountability looks like in practice, one must examine not intentions, but structures.

Accountability Is Not Compliance

In contemporary urban governance, accountability is often reduced to compliance. Housing agencies meet federal reporting requirements. Developers satisfy affordability set-

---

[1] Schuyler Louie, John Mondragon, Rami Najjar, and Johannes F. Wieland, "Housing Affordability and Housing Demand," *FRBSF Economic Letter* 2026-03 (February 2, 2026), https://www.frbsf.org/research-and-insights/publications/economic-letter/2026/02/housing-affordability-and-housing-demand/

asides. Cities publish dashboards and performance indicators. Yet compliance ensures procedural correctness, not necessarily substantive results.

Compliance-based accountability asks whether rules were followed, not whether harm was avoided. A project can meet affordability mandates and still accelerate neighborhood-wide displacement. It can satisfy ESG benchmarks while weakening long-term housing stability. This distinction matters: compliance regulates conduct within the system, while accountability evaluates whether the system is producing its stated public purposes.

Chicago's redevelopment initiatives illustrate this dynamic. Projects met inclusionary zoning requirements and bond covenants, yet surrounding neighborhoods experienced rapid rent escalation. No rule was broken, but stated public goals were not met.[2]

Power Determines Where Accountability Lands

True accountability follows power. In urban development, power is concentrated upstream— in capital markets, monetary policy, bond structures, and land control. Yet accountability mechanisms are disproportionately applied downstream, to housing agencies, nonprofit developers, and residents.

Housing agencies are audited. Residents are means-tested. Community organizations are monitored for compliance. By contrast, speculative capital flows, interest-rate shocks, and

---

[2] Illinois Policy Institute, *Report: Chicago Lost Out on 43,000 Homes Because of Zoning Mandates*, press release, October 1, 2025, https://www.illinoispolicy.org/press-releases/report-chicago-lost-out-on-43000-homes-because-of-zoning-mandates/

land value appreciation remain largely outside accountability frameworks. The result is a moral inversion: those with the least control face the most scrutiny.[3]

This asymmetry is visible across cities. In Los Angeles, housing agencies are held responsible for affordability shortfalls while operating within land markets shaped by global capital. For example, as of August 2025, Los Angeles County saw a dramatic decline in housing production from 70,000 units annually in the 1950s to less than 15,000 in recent years. Between 2018 and 2024, only 10% of new housing units were certified as affordable to lower-income households, even as agencies faced mounting pressure to deliver results.[4] In Detroit, residents are asked to adapt to redevelopment strategies over which they had minimal influence. Accountability becomes a mechanism for managing legitimacy rather than redistributing power. For example, the City of Detroit proposed the 2025-2030 Detroit Affordable Housing Strategy aims to preserve 10,000 units and construct 3,000 new ones, yet these plans are largely top-down initiatives managed by the Housing and Revitalization

---

[3] David M. Greenberg, Julia Duranti-Martínez, Francisca Winston, Spenser Anderson, Jacob Udell, Caroline Kirk, and Richard D. Hendra, "Housing Speculation, Affordable Investments, and Tenant Outcomes in New York City," *Cityscape: A Journal of Policy Development and Research* 26, no. 1 (2024): 153–77, U.S. Department of Housing and Urban Development, Office of Policy Development and Research, https://www.huduser.gov/portal/periodicals/cityscape/vol26num1/ch8.pdf

[4] USC Price School of Public Policy, Report: L.A. Housing Demand Increases Despite Population Declines, January 31, 2025, https://priceschool.usc.edu/news/los-angeles-la-housing-crisis-data-homelessness/

Department.[5] As altruistic and optimistic as these proposals are, they all operate under the mechanism of municipal financial structure which are governed by municipal credit agencies, underwriters, banks, private equity firms, hedge funds, developers and private interests because investment into a city is highly influenced by the credit ratings of a city in the municipal bond market.

Temporal Accountability and the Problem of Short Horizons

Most accountability frameworks operate on short timelines. Compliance periods last 15 to 30 years. Political cycles last four. Investor return horizons are often shorter still. Displacement and housing insecurity, by contrast, unfold over generations.

Accountability measured over the short-term permits projects to register success while postponing the consequences that unfold over the long term. Affordability covenants lapse, oversight mechanisms expire, and neighborhood transformations accelerate once public obligations are no longer enforced. Such temporal asymmetries enable municipalities and investors to internalize immediate benefits while externalizing future costs.[6]

---

[5] City of Detroit Housing and Revitalization Department, *2025–2030 Detroit Affordable Housing Strategy* (Detroit: City of Detroit, 2025), https://detroitmi.gov/sites/detroitmi.localhost/files/2025-08/Detroit%20Market%20Housing%20Strategy%20(Digital).pdf

[6] Rachel G. Bratt, Michael E. Stone, and Chester W. Hartman, eds., *A Right to Housing: Foundation for a New Social Agenda* (Philadelphia: Temple University Press, 2006).

What Accountability Looks Like in Practice?

Baltimore's redevelopment history reflects this pattern. Projects initially framed as stabilizing investments met their formal obligations, only for affordability protections to dissolve as market pressures intensified. The accountability clock expired before residents experienced lasting security.

Accountability Without Enforcement Is Narrative

Public engagement processes are often treated as evidence of accountability. Community meetings, advisory boards, and public comment periods create forums for expression, but they rarely alter the financial architecture of a project.

Participation without enforcement risks becoming performative. Residents are heard but not empowered. Feedback is recorded but not binding. Development legitimacy is sustained through procedural inclusion rather than material outcome. As Keeanga-Yamahtta Taylor demonstrates, formal inclusion within a system does not necessarily translate into equitable access to its benefits.[7]

In Jersey City, extensive public consultation accompanied major redevelopment initiatives, yet affordability thresholds, underwriting assumptions and financial structures remained largely unchanged. The appearance of accountability substituted for meaningful constraint.

Fiscal Accountability and the Hidden Trade-Offs

Cities frequently frame accountability in fiscal terms: balanced budgets, bond ratings, and creditworthiness. These metrics matter, but they are incomplete. Fiscal

---

[7] Keeanga-Yamahtta Taylor, *Race for Profit: How Banks and the Real Estate Industry Undermined Black Homeownership* (Chapel Hill: University of North Carolina Press, 2019).

accountability prioritizes the city's relationship with capital markets over its relationship with residents.

Maintaining bond ratings can constrain policy choices, discouraging rent stabilization, land banking, or long-term public ownership. These trade-offs are rarely made explicit. Market discipline is presented as neutral necessity rather than political choice.[8]

Philadelphia's property-tax abatements illustrate this tension. While proponents argue abatements can stabilize neighborhoods and eventually generate revenue, benefits have been highly concentrated. In 2017, a majority of abatement value accrued to a small fraction of neighborhoods. The policy's distributive consequences were largely absent from accountability discussions.[9][10]

Structural Accountability: Aligning Risk and Reward

Meaningful accountability requires aligning risk with reward. In current systems, public actors absorb risk while private actors capture upside. Most accountability frameworks leave this imbalance intact.

---

[8] Amy T. Khare, "Market-Driven Public Housing Reforms: Inadequacy for Poverty Alleviation," *Cityscape: A Journal of Policy Development and Research* 15, no. 2 (2013): 193–204, U.S. Department of Housing and Urban Development https://www.huduser.gov/portal/periodicals/cityscpe/vol15num2/ch13.pdf

[9] Tobias Peter, "Philadelphia's Property Tax Abatement Success Story," *City Journal*, accessed February 3, 2026, https://www.city-journal.org/article/philadelphia-revival-property-tax-abatement.

[10] Dina Bleckman, "Unpacking the Real Estate Tax Abatement Debate," *Temple 10-Q*, Temple University Beasley School of Law, May�??�202X, https://law.temple.edu/10q/unpacking-the-real-estate-tax-abatement-debate/

What Accountability Looks Like in Practice?

Structural accountability demands that beneficiaries of public de-risking also bear responsibility for social outcomes. This can include permanent affordability requirements tied to subsidies, shared-equity models, land-value recapture, and enforceable *clawback* provisions when public objectives are not met.

Cities that invest in community land trusts and long-term public land stewardship move closer to this model. By retaining control over land, they extend accountability beyond project timelines and insulate housing from speculative pressures.

Measuring What Actually Matters

If accountability is to be meaningful, it must measure outcomes that reflect lived experience: displacement rates, rent-burden trajectories, demographic continuity, and long-term housing security.

These metrics are more complex—and more politically uncomfortable—than unit counts or investment totals. They require confronting distributional consequences rather than aggregate growth. Without them, accountability remains abstract.

Chicago's emerging neighborhood-level displacement tracking offers a partial model, demonstrating that accountability can evolve when political will aligns with analytic capacity.

Accountability as Institutional Design

Accountability is not a moral posture. It is an institutional design choice. Cities decide whom to protect, what to measure, and which risks to tolerate. These choices shape urban outcomes more powerfully than any individual project.

When accountability is embedded structurally through land control, long-term affordability, and aligned incentives—it becomes enforceable. When it remains procedural, it becomes symbolic. The difference determines whether development stabilizes communities or merely passes through them.

From Blame to Responsibility

This framework shifts accountability away from blame and toward responsibility. Housing agencies are not villains. Investors are not inherently predatory. Cities are not uniquely negligent. Each operates within a system that rewards certain behaviors and penalizes others.

True accountability asks not who failed, but which structures produced predictable outcomes—and how those structures can be redesigned. This shift is essential if urban development is to move beyond cyclical crisis management toward sustained stability.

The Conditions for Credible Accountability

For accountability to function effectively, it must meet three criteria: it must be congruent with established power relations, persist over time, and be enforced through institutional mechanisms rather than dependent on goodwill or sentiment.

Absent these conditions, accountability remains rhetorical—present in speeches, reports, and frameworks but absent where it matters most: in the long-term stability of neighborhoods and the security of residents.

In practice, accountability is not about perfect outcomes; it is about designing systems in which harm is harder to externalize, responsibility follows benefit, and urban development serves continuity rather than displacement.

CHAPTER 11: Stabilization is Not Stagnation

In urban policy discourse, stabilization is often treated as a concession—a pause imposed on growth to manage its excesses. It is framed as a defensive response to market forces rather than a proactive development strategy. This framing misunderstands both the nature of urban growth and the role stability plays in sustaining it. Stability is not the absence of change. It is the condition that allows change to occur without systemic harm.

When cities fail to stabilize housing markets and communities, they do not accelerate progress; they introduce volatility that ultimately undermines economic productivity, political legitimacy, and social cohesion. Instability does not signal dynamism. It signals fragility.

This chapter argues that stabilization is a prerequisite for durable urban development. It is not an ideological stance nor an anti-market position, it is a structural recognition of how cities actually function over time. Growth that is not anchored by stability becomes extractive—generating short-term gains while eroding long-term capacity. Stability, properly designed, transforms growth from a zero-sum process into a cumulative one.

The False Opposition Between Growth and Protection

Urban development debates frequently frame cities as facing a binary choice: encourage growth or protect residents. This framing obscures a critical reality: unprotected growth produces instability that eventually constrains further development.

Housing insecurity, displacement, and rapid neighborhood turnover weaken labor markets, disrupt education systems, strain public services, and generate political resistance that slows or halts new projects. Volatility undermines investor confidence just as surely as regulation does.

Cities such as New York, San Francisco, and Los Angeles illustrate this contradiction. Despite extraordinary levels of capital investment, these cities continue to face chronic housing shortages, declining affordability, and escalating opposition to development. Growth has occurred, but it has not translated into stability. Instead, scarcity has intensified, political polarization has hardened, and development processes have grown more contested.[1]

The problem is not excessive growth; it is growth without sufficient stabilizing mechanisms. By contrast, cities that embed protections early—before markets overheat—experience less volatility and more predictable development trajectories. Stability is not the enemy of growth. Unmanaged growth is the enemy of stability.

Stability as Urban Economic Infrastructure

Housing stability functions as a form of economic infrastructure, as essential to urban productivity as transportation, utilities or digital connectivity. Stable housing allows near employment centers, children to stay in schools, and small businesses to retain customer bases. It reduces friction across labor, education, and service systems.

When housing becomes unstable, cities incur costs that rarely appear in development budgets but accumulate across public systems. Research consistently links displacement

---

[1] Richard Florida, *The New Urban Crisis* (New York: Basic Books, 2017).

and housing insecurity to increased healthcare utilization, mental health strain, educational disruption, and reduced long-term earnings.[2] These outcomes are not incidental side effects; they are structural consequences of instability.[3]

Cities that tolerate housing volatility externalize costs onto schools, hospitals, emergency services, and social programs. In effect, they subsidize market inefficiency by absorbing the downstream consequences of upstream financial decisions.

Stability therefore operates as a multiplier. It reduces public expenditure volatility, strengthens workforce continuity, and supports intergenerational wealth retention. Its absence generates cascading inefficiencies that undermine both equity and growth.

Stability as a Development Strategy

The case of Detroit offers a useful illustration. Neighborhoods that experienced stabilization through targeted interventions—property tax relief, repair assistance, and long-term affordability protections—demonstrated stronger recovery outcomes than areas subjected primarily to speculative turnover.[4]

---

[2] Sungwoo Lim, Pui Ying Chan, Sarah Walters, Gretchen Culp, Mary Huynh, and L. Hannah Gould, "Impact of Residential Displacement on Healthcare Access and Mental Health among Original Residents of Gentrifying Neighborhoods in New York City," PLoS ONE 12, no. 12 (December 22, 2017): e0190139, https://doi.org/10.1371/journal.pone.0190139.

[3] Lim et al., "Impact of Residential Displacement," e0190139.

[4] Lydia Wileden, *Evaluating Variation in Neighborhood Sentiments Among Strategic Neighborhood Fund Residents* (*DMACS Wave 17, Summer 2023*) (Detroit: Detroit Metro Area Communities Study, June

Where residents were able to remain and participate in neighborhood change, investment produced cumulative gains. Social networks endured. Local demand stabilized. Small businesses survived long enough to benefit from rising foot traffic. Stability amplified recovery.

By contrast, neighborhoods characterized by rapid churn experienced repeated cycles of speculation and vacancy. Capital arrived, extracted value, and retreated. Physical redevelopment occurred, but social and economic continuity did not.

The lesson is not that markets must be frozen. It is that growth requires anchoring. Without stabilization mechanisms, capital movement generates oscillation rather than development.

Reframing Stabilization

Stabilization should not be understood as rent freezes alone, nor as temporary relief during crises. It encompasses a broader toolkit: durable affordability covenants, public land stewardship, predictable property taxation, anti-displacement protections, and financing structures that reward long-term occupancy over short-term turnover.

These mechanisms reduce volatility without suppressing investment. They create conditions under which growth compounds rather than displaces. They align private return with public continuity.

Stability, in this sense, is not restraint. It is governance.

2024), https://detroitsurvey.umich.edu/wp-content/uploads/2024/07/DMACS-SNF-Wave-17-FINAL.pdf

Stability and Long-term Urban Competitiveness

Cities compete not only for capital but for labor, families, and institutional trust. Housing volatility erodes all three. When residents cannot predict whether they will remain in their homes, they delay investment in community, education, and local enterprise. Employers face higher turnover. Schools lose continuity. Civic participation declines.

Long-term competitiveness depends on predictability. Stability lowers transaction costs across the urban system. It reduces resistance to new development because residents are less fearful of displacement. It transforms growth from threat to opportunity.

The choice is not between growth and protection. It is between volatility and durability.

Stabilization is therefore not a concession to political pressure. It is the foundation of resilient urban development. Cities that recognize this, design for continuity rather than for crisis. Those that do not remain trapped in cycles of boom, backlash, and retrenchment.

The next question, then, is not whether stabilization slows growth. It is how cities can institutionalize stability so that growth strengthens rather than destabilizes the communities on which it depends.

Stabilization as Risk Management, Not Regulation

Stabilization should be understood not as restriction, but as risk management. Volatile housing markets introduce uncertainty into municipal budgets, bond ratings, labor markets and long-term planning. Sudden rent increases, displacement, and population churn destabilize tax bases, strain public services and generate political backlash that ultimately increases development risk.

Stabilization tools—long-term affordability covenants, community land trusts, and tenant protections—reduce this volatility. They smooth market cycles and create conditions under which development can proceed without triggering social fracture. While these tools may constrain speculative upside, they significantly reduce systemic downside risk.[5]

Increasingly, investors recognize that extreme volatility undermines long-term asset value. Markets characterized by rapid displacement and recurring political backlash become less predictable, raising regulatory, reputational, and litigation risk. Stabilization aligns urban development with longer investment horizons, favoring patient capital over opportunistic extraction.

Properly designed, stabilization does not interfere with markets. It disciplines instability.

Rethinking Rent Stabilization

Rent stabilization remains one of the most misunderstood tools in urban development. Critics portray it as a blunt price control that discourages investment and degrades housing quality. Yet empirical research demonstrates that outcomes vary substantially depending on design, enforcement, and integration with broader housing policy.

---

[5] Jakob Kendall Schneider, Mary Clare Lennon, and Susan Saegert, "Do Community Land Trusts Improve Resident Outcomes?" *Housing Matters* (Urban Institute, February 21, 2024), https://housingmatters.urban.org/research-summary/do-community-land-trusts-improve-resident-outcomes

Effective rent stabilization systems typically include maintenance cost recovery mechanisms, capital improvement pass-throughs, exemptions or phased treatment for new construction, adjustments tied to inflation or operating costs, and strong enforcement against abuse. When integrated with supply expansion and small-landlord support, rent stabilization can protect tenants from displacement without systematically suppressing new investment.

Policy failure in this area typically reflects reactive implementation rather than inherent flaw. When stabilization is introduced as emergency politics rather than as institutional infrastructure, it becomes symbolic rather than systemic. Cities that treat stabilization as governance architecture—not ideological signaling—achieve more balanced outcomes.

Permanence as the Missing Dimension of Affordability

Affordability that expires is not stability; it is postponement.

Numerous housing programs operate under time-limited compliance frameworks. Low-Income Housing Tax Credit (LIHTC) units, for instance, are governed by a 30-year affordability mandate, consisting of a 15-year initial compliance period and a subsequent 15-year extended-use period. Beyond this term, units may convert to market-rate housing unless further subsidies or regulatory restrictions are enacted.[6]

---

[6] Maxwell Jaffe and Dustin Ingram, *"Expirations and Early Exits of LIHTC Units: Implications for the Affordable Housing Stock,"* Chicago Fed Letter no. 514 (October 16 2025), Federal Reserve Bank of Chicago, https://www.chicagofed.org/publications/chicago-fed-letter/2025/514

Time-limited affordability protects households temporarily but does not remove housing from speculative cycles. When compliance periods lapse during periods of market pressure, displacement resumes.

Permanent affordability mechanisms operate differently. Community land trusts, deed restrictions with perpetual terms, public land ownership and shared-equity models remove land from speculative markets and preserve affordability across generations. These structures separate land value from housing value, ensuring that gains are recycled into long-term community benefit rather than extracted through appreciation.[78]

Cities that invest in permanence reduce the need for continual subsidy rounds. Rather than chasing affordability reactively, they construct durable housing ecosystems that retain value for residents and municipalities alike.

Permanence lowers volatility across decades.

Stabilization and Democratic Legitimacy

Urban development is as much political as it is economic. Perceived destabilization among residents undermines trust, intensifies opposition, increases litigation, and prolongs project timelines.

---

[7] Joseph Schilling, Samantha Fu, and Yonah Freemark, Promoting Equitable Development in Communities: *An Overview of Five Promising Strategies* (Washington, DC: Urban Institute, June 2024), https://www.urban.org/sites/default/files/2024-06/Promoting_Equitable_Development_in_Communities.pdf

[8] Schilling, Fu, and Freemark, *Promoting Equitable Development*

Stabilization is Not Stagnation

Stabilization restores democratic legitimacy by signaling that residents are not expendable inputs to growth. When people believe they can remain in place, participation shifts from resistance to collaboration.

This legitimacy produces measurable effects. Cities with credible anti-displacement frameworks face less political friction and greater flexibility in advancing ambitious projects. Stability lowers the political cost of growth.

The Hidden Costs of Instability

Instability generates costs rarely attributed to development policy. Displacement disrupts informal care networks, weakens community-based institutions, and erodes social capital. These losses accumulate over time and are difficult to rebuild.

From a municipal perspective, instability creates fiscal inefficiency. Cities repeatedly invest in infrastructure and revitalization only to lose residents and institutional continuity. Stabilization protects not just households, but prior public investment.[9]

When these downstream costs are excluded from evaluation, development appears more profitable than it truly is. Stabilization corrects this distortion by internalizing long-term consequences.

Stabilization as a Platform for Inclusive Growth

Stabilization does not preclude growth; it shapes its trajectory. Stable neighborhoods support entrepreneurship, workforce participation, and local wealth-building. When

---

[9] Keeanga-Yamahtta Taylor, *Race for Profit* (Chapel Hill: University of North Carolina Press, 2019).

residents are not consumed by housing insecurity, they are more likely to invest in community life and economic activity.

Inclusive growth depends on continuity. Businesses require stable customer bases. Schools require stable enrollment. Civic institutions require long-term participation.

Stabilization allows growth to compound rather than reset.

Scaling Stabilization Through Institutions

The question for cities is not whether stabilization works, but how to embed it structurally. Fragmented measures fail against systemic market pressure. Stabilization must be integrated into:

- Land use policy
- Housing finance structures
- Bond frameworks
- Redevelopment mandates
- Public land stewardship

Bond covenants, agency mandates, and investment criteria must align with long-term stability goals. Stabilization cannot remain exceptional; it must become standard practice.

Stability as Governance

Stabilization reframes urban development from restraint to design. The question is not how much growth cities can tolerate, but how growth can reinforce continuity rather than disrupt it.

This reframing dissolves the perceived conflict between residents and investors. Stability benefits both. Cities that

Stabilization is Not Stagnation

understand this attract patient capital and sustain durable prosperity.

Stabilization is not charity. It is governance.

Growth succeeds when it reinforces belonging rather than replacing it.

CONCLUSION

The Question Every City Must Answer

Cities do not fail for lack of ambition. They falter when the systems through which they pursue development are structurally misaligned with the outcomes they claim to seek.

Throughout this book, I have argued that contemporary urban instability—housing precarity, displacement, fiscal fragility, social fragmentation—is not the product of cultural dysfunction or municipal incompetence. It is the predictable outcome of financial and institutional arrangements that prioritize liquidity, risk transfer, and short-term performance over long-term stability.

At the center of this misalignment lies a financial chain that begins beyond the city. Federal monetary policy shapes credit conditions, risk appetites, and asset valuations. These conditions flow into the municipal bond market, where cities finance basic governance and redevelopment. Capital is then channeled through housing authorities, redevelopment agencies, and public-private partnerships operating within market logics.

By the time development reaches the neighborhood, the terms have already been set.

Displacement, austerity, and exclusion are not unintended byproducts. They are structurally embedded consequences of systems designed to protect capital and preserve liquidity.

The Double Bind

Cities face a persistent double bind.

They are tasked with delivering affordability, equity, and stability. Yet they remain dependent on financial instruments that reward scarcity, turnover, and appreciation.

Housing agencies are asked to preserve affordability while underwriting deals that require rising rents. Redevelopment authorities are charged with revitalization while operating within debt structures that demand revenue growth. Local officials are evaluated on fiscal solvency while constrained by bond markets and policy regimes beyond their control.

Risk is not eliminated. It is relocated—downward and outward.

Displacement is not policy failure. It is systemic execution.

Racial Capitalism and Financial Imperialism

These dynamics are inseparable from the history of racial capitalism. Black and low-income communities have long functioned as sites where financial experimentation, extraction, and risk displacement are absorbed most readily. Redlining, urban renewal, subprime lending, and contemporary speculative redevelopment differ in form but share structural logic: selective exposure of marginalized populations to volatility in service of broader financial stability.

Financial imperialism clarifies this further. Just as global South economies operate under external monetary regimes and debt discipline, many U.S. cities—particularly those with constrained tax bases—operate within analogous systems of financial dependency. Access to capital is conditional. Policy autonomy is constrained. Development trajectories are shaped less by democratic preference than by feasibility as defined by markets.

The parallels are structural, not metaphorical.

The Limits of ESG

The rise of ESG and impact investing has introduced new language of responsibility but has not altered underlying incentive structures. Metrics are often decoupled from material outcomes. Accountability remains diffuse. Disclosure substitutes for redesign.

ESG frequently legitimizes extractive arrangements rather than transforming them.

What Must Change

Sustainable development cannot be achieved through better branding or incremental regulation. It requires structural realignment.

- Stability must be treated as a public asset.
- Housing must be governed as infrastructure.
- Accountability must extend beyond local agencies to financial architectures.
- Risk and reward must be aligned.
- Permanence must replace temporary mitigation.

Cities need not disengage from capital markets. But they must renegotiate their role within them.

Development must be evaluated not by units delivered or dollars invested, but by whether communities are more secure, more stable, and more resilient over time.

The Question

The question every city must answer is not whether it wants growth.

The question is:

Who bears the risk? Specifically;

- Who captures the upside?
- Who is protected when markets shift?

Until cities confront this honestly—and restructure institutions accordingly—displacement will continue to be described as unfortunate even as it remains predictable.

The future of urban development will not be determined by intention, but by institutional design.

Cities must decide whether they will remain intermediaries for financial systems—or stewards of collective stability.

That choice is monetary.
It is institutional.
And it is profoundly political.

This reality places cities in a persistent double bind. On the one hand, they are tasked with delivering affordability, equity, and stability. On the other, they are structurally dependent on financial instruments, investors, and development models that reward scarcity, turnover, and appreciation. Housing agencies are asked to preserve affordability while underwriting deals that require rising rents. Redevelopment authorities are charged with revitalization while operating within debt structures that demand revenue growth. Local officials are evaluated on fiscal solvency while constrained by bond ratings, capital markets, and federal policy regimes over which they have little control.

In this context, risk is never eliminated—it is merely relocated. Fiscal risk is transferred from federal institutions to cities, from cities to redevelopment agencies, from agencies to residents. Financial volatility becomes spatialized, embedded in neighborhoods where rising costs, precarious tenure, and uneven investment become normalized features of urban life. Displacement, then, is not the failure of policy intention; it is the successful execution of a system designed to prioritize financial performance over social continuity.

Importantly, this book does not argue against markets, investment, or private capital. Nor does it romanticize stagnation or oppose growth. Rather, it challenges the assumption that current financial arrangements are neutral, inevitable, or efficient in delivering public goods. The problem is not that cities engage with capital, but that they do so on terms that systematically subordinate long-term residents, public agencies, and social objectives to the imperatives of liquidity and return.

What this book ultimately argues is not that cities should reject investment, growth, or financial participation, but that they must confront the asymmetries embedded in their current position. Sustainable development cannot be achieved so long as cities remain structurally responsible for social outcomes while being financially constrained by systems designed elsewhere. Stability must be treated as a public asset worthy of protection, not as inefficiency to be engineered away. Housing must be governed as infrastructure, not merely as an investment class. And accountability must extend beyond local agencies to the financial architectures that shape their choices.

The question every city must answer, then, is not simply how to grow or whom to attract, but how much instability it is willing to absorb on behalf of the financial system, and who is expected to bear that cost. Until this question is addressed at the level of monetary policy, capital markets, and institutional design, displacement will continue to be framed as unintended—even as it remains structurally necessary.

The future of urban development will be determined not by better intentions, but by whether cities can reclaim meaningful agency within the financial systems that govern them. That challenge is not merely municipal. It is monetary, institutional, and fundamentally political.

These dynamics cannot be fully understood without acknowledging the role of racial capitalism in structuring urban development. Historically marginalized communities—particularly Black, Latinx and low-income neighborhoods—have long served as sites where financial experimentation, extraction, and risk displacement are most easily absorbed. Redlining, urban renewal, subprime lending, and contemporary forms of speculative redevelopment differ in form but share a common function: the selective exposure of certain populations to market volatility in the service of broader financial stability. Displacement, in this sense, is not merely a housing issue; it is a mechanism through which systemic risk is spatially and socially redistributed.

Financial imperialism further clarifies this process. Just as global South economies have been conditioned by external monetary regimes, debt dependence, and capital discipline, U.S. cities—particularly those with constrained tax bases—operate under analogous forms of financial subordination. Access to capital is contingent, conditional, and costly. Policy autonomy is limited by market expectations, and development trajectories are shaped less by democratic preference than by financial feasibility. The parallels are not rhetorical; they reflect shared structural logics of dependency and control.

The growing reliance on ESG frameworks and impact narratives has not resolved this contradiction. While these tools have introduced a new language of responsibility into investment discourse, they have largely failed to alter underlying incentive structures. Metrics are often decoupled from material outcomes, accountability is diffuse, and success is measured by disclosure rather than by durability. As a result, ESG frequently legitimizes extractive practices rather than constraining them, offering cities reputational cover without structural change.

What emerges from this analysis is a clear conclusion: sustainable development cannot be achieved through isolated projects, better branding, or marginal regulatory tweaks. It requires a fundamental reorientation of how cities define success, manage risk, and structure accountability. Stability must be treated not as an obstacle to growth, but as a public good in its own right. Affordability must be protected not only at the point of development, but across the financial life cycle of housing assets. Public institutions must be empowered to act as stewards of long-term value rather than as intermediaries for short-term capital flows.

This does not mean cities must disengage from capital markets. It means they must renegotiate their role within them. Accountability must be embedded in financing structures, not appended through reporting requirements. Public agencies must retain meaningful control over land, affordability covenants, and governance mechanisms. Development must be evaluated not solely by units delivered or dollars invested, but by whether communities are more secure, more stable, and more resilient over time.

Ultimately, the question every city must answer is not whether it wants growth, investment, or revitalization. The question is who bears the risk, who captures the upside, and who is protected when market conditions shift. Until cities confront this question honestly—and restructure their institutions accordingly—displacement will continue to be framed as an unfortunate consequence rather than recognized as a financial outcome.

The future of urban development will not be determined by ambition alone, but by whether cities are willing to align their financial systems with their public purpose. That choice, more than any individual project or policy, will define whether cities remain engines of shared prosperity or mechanisms for managed exclusion.

References

Aalbers, Manuel B. *The Financialization of Housing: A Political Economy Approach*. London: Routledge, 2016. https://doi.org/10.4324/9781315668666.

Abatement Addiction: A Case Study on Jersey City's Municipal Tax Abatements, Urban Gentrification and the Politics of Rights. Paper presented at the APSA 2011 Annual Meeting. SSRN, 2011. https://papers.ssrn.com/sol3/papers.cfm?abstract_id=1901269.

Adelman, Jacob. "Philly's 'Opportunity Zone' Tracts Are Some of the City's Poorest, and among Its Biggest Gentrifiers, Fed Finds." *The Philadelphia Inquirer*, November 15, 2019. https://www.inquirer.com/real-estate/commercial/opportunity-zones-philadelphia-federal-reserve-gentrification-poverty-development-20191115.html.

Alliance, Pilsen. "NO Pilsen TIF Expansion! — Pilsen Alliance." *Pilsen Alliance*, July 16, 2024. https://www.thepilsenalliance.org/news-and-events/no-pilsen-tif-expansion.

Alroy, Karen, A, Aldo Crossa, Shu Wang M, and Sze Liu Y. *Can Changing Neighborhoods Influence Mental Health? An Ecological Analysis of Gentrification and Neighborhood-Level Serious Psychological Distress—New York City, 2002–2015*. Department of Public Health Scholarship and Creative Works, Montclair State University, 2023.

https://digitalcommons.montclair.edu/cgi/viewcontent.cgi?article=1220&context=public-health-facpubs.

Atlanta Wealth Building Initiative. *Building a Beloved Economy: A Baseline and Framework for Building Black Wealth in Atlanta.* Atlanta Wealth Building Initiative, 2023. https://buildblackwealth.info/2023/10/AWBI-BuildingABelovedEconomy-Final.pdf.

ATLbudget. "The People's Guide to the City of Atlanta's Budget." ATLbudget. Accessed March 20, 2026. https://atlbudget.org/.

Blyth, Mark. *Austerity: The History of a Dangerous Idea.* New York: Oxford University Press, 2013.

Boadi, Kwame. *Making Sense of the District's Tax Abatement Dollars: Nine Questions to Consider.* Washington, DC: DC Fiscal Policy Institute, December 14, 2011.

Boyd, Mike. "Trio Secures $575M for Centennial Yards." Connect CRE, 1,. https://www.connectcre.com/stories/trio-secures-575m-for-centennial-yards/.

Bratt, Rachel G., Michael E. Stone, and Chester W. Hartman, eds. *A Right to Housing: Foundation for a New Social Agenda.* Philadelphia: Temple University Press, 2006.

CBS Boston. "Report: Boston Is 3rd 'Most Intensely Gentrified City' In America." *CBS Boston*, July 8, 2020. https://www.cbsnews.com/boston/news/boston-gentrification-study-cities-report/.

Center for Civic Innovation. *FY 2026 Organizer's Guide to the City of Atlanta Budget*. Center for Civic Innovation, 2025. https://atlbudget.org/wp-content/uploads/2025/05/FY2026-Organizers-Guide-to-the-City-of-Atlanta-Budget.pdf.

Center on Budget and Policy Priorities. *Public Housing: Policy Basics*. Washington, DC, updated September 30, 2024.

City of Atlanta. *Affordable Housing Strike Force Update*. City of Atlanta, 2024. https://www.atlantaga.gov/home/showpublisheddocument/64358/638736596596500000.

City of Chicago Office of the CFO. *Bond Rating Outlook Downgrade*. Chicago, November 6, 2025.

City of Chicago, . *Tax Increment Financing (TIF) Program Guide 2020* . City of Chicago Department of Planning and Development, 2020. https://www.chicago.gov/content/dam/city/depts/dcd/general/2020_tif_program_guide.pdf.

City of Chicago. *Mayor Brandon Johnson Presents the Protecting Chicago Budget Proposal for Fiscal Year 2025*. City of Chicago Office of the Mayor, 2025. https://www.chicago.gov/city/en/depts/mayor/press_room/press_releases/2025/october/budget-proposal-2025.html.

City of Chicago. *TIF District Programming 2021-2025*. City of Chicago, Department of Planning and Development, 2021. https://www.chicago.gov/content/dam/city/depts/dcd/tif/projections/TIF_District_Programming_2021_2025.pdf.

City of Detroit Housing and Revitalization Department. *2025–2030 Detroit Affordable Housing Strategy*. Detroit, 2025.

City of Jersey City. "Mayor Introduces Inclusionary Zoning Ordinance." Press release, November 19, 2021.

City of Los Angeles Department of City Planning. *Housing Element 2021–2029: Chapter 2—Constraints on Housing Maintenance, Improvement, and Development*. Los Angeles, 2025.

———. *Project Determination Document*, Case No. MTY1MDK0. Los Angeles, 2025.

City of New York Office of Management and Budget. *Fiscal Year 2026–2035 Ten-Year Capital Strategy*. New York, 2025.

Cohen, Steven. "A Quarter of the 21st Century Over: What We've Learned about Sustainability and What Might Be Next." Columbia University School of Professional Studies, December 29, 2025.

Collins, Sam, P.K. "The U Street Corridor: Past Glory, Present-Day Questions." *The Washington Informer*, February 20, 2026. https://www.washingtoninformer.com/u-street-housing-affordability-concerns/.

Competitive Enterprise Institute. *Environmental, Social, and Governance Theory*. Washington, DC, 2025.

Connors, Chris. "50 Years Broken Promises and Record Flooding for Morristown." *Morristown Minute*, September 15, 2021.

https://morristownminute.town.news/g/morristown-nj/n/41748/50-years-broken-promises-and-record-flooding-morristown.

CRE Daily. "CIM Taps $556M in Muni Bonds to Fund $4.2B Atlanta Project." August 16, 2024. https://www.credaily.com/briefs/cim-taps-556-million-dollars-in-muni-bonds-to-fund-4-2-billion-dollar-atlanta-project.

Data USA. "Hoboken, NJ – Profile." Data USA. Accessed February 21, 2026. https://datausa.io/profile/geo/hoboken-nj?redirect=true.

Desmond, Matthew. *Evicted: Poverty and Profit in the American City*. Crown Publishers, 2016.

Digital Scholarship Lab, University of Richmond. "Mapping Inequality: Redlining in New Deal America." Accessed February 21, 2026. https://dsl.richmond.edu/panorama/redlining/map#loc=4/40.4939/-95.8425.

Digital Scholarship Lab, University of Richmond. *Mapping Inequality*. 2026. https://dsl.richmond.edu/panorama/redlining/map.

Digital Scholarship Lab, University of Richmond. *Mapping Inequality: Redlining in New Deal America*. New Jersey, 2026. D27□—□Hudson County. https://dsl.richmond.edu/panorama/redlining/map/NJ/HudsonCo/area_descriptions/D27#mapview=full&loc=15/40.7097/-74.0526.

Ding, Lei, Jackelyn Hwang, and Eileen Divringi. "Gentrification and Residential Mobility in Philadelphia."

Regional Science and Urban Economics 61 (September 2016): 38–51.
https://doi.org/10.1016/j.regsciurbeco.2016.09.004.

Draper, Elaine. Review of *Risk, Society, and Social Theory*, by Ulrich Beck, Mark Ritter, and Mary Douglas. *Contemporary Sociology* 22, no. 5 (1993): 641–644.

Econsult Corporation, Penn Institute for Urban Research, and May 8 Consulting. *Vacant Land Management in Philadelphia: The Costs of the Current System and the Benefits of Reform*. Philadelphia, March 17, 2010.

Ehlenz, Meagan, M. "Can You Imagine What's Happened in Durham?': Duke University and a New University–Community Engagement Model." *Journal of the American Planning Association* 87, no. 1 (2020): 45 - 61. https://doi.org/10.1080/01944363.2020.1782766.

Ehlenz, Meagan, M. *Universities and Affordable Housing: Seven Case Studies*. Penn Institute for Urban Research, 2023. https://penniur.upenn.edu/publications/universities-and-affordable-housing-seven-case-studies.

Fainstein, Susan S. "The Just City." *International Journal of Urban Sciences* 18, no. 1 (2014): 1–18.

Federal Reserve Bank of Philadelphia. "Philadelphia Fed Research Measures Impact of Gentrification on Low-Cost Housing Stock." Federal Reserve Bank of Philadelphia Community Development, December 19, 2016. https://www.philadelphiafed.org/community-development/housing-and-neighborhoods/philadelphia-fed-research-measures-impact-of-gentrification-on-low-cost-housing-stock.

Federal Reserve Bank of Philadelphia. *How Are Cities Leveraging Opportunity Zones for Community Development?* Federal Reserve Bank of Philadelphia, 2019. https://www.philadelphiafed.org/-/media/frbp/assets/community-development/reports/1119-opportunity-zones.pdf.

Fernandez, Rodrigo. "Financialization and Housing: Between Globalization and Varieties of Capitalism." In *The Financialization of Housing*, edited by Manuel B. Aalbers, 97–116. London: Routledge, 2016.

Fitzsimmons, Emma. "Hudson Yards and the New New York." New York Times, March 18, 2019. https://www.nytimes.com/2019/03/18/nyregion/newyorktoday/nyc-news-hudson-yards.html.

Florida, Richard. *The New Urban Crisis*. New York: Basic Books, 2017.

Foretek, Jared. "The Story of the Pittsburgh Neighborhood That Inspired 'Fences.'" In *Saving Places*. National Trust for Historic Preservation, 2017. https://savingplaces.org/stories/the-story-of-the-pittsburgh-neighborhood-that-inspired-fences.

Freemark, Yonah, Mel Langness, Amanda Hermans, Gabe Samuels, Tomi Rajninger, and David Blount. *Is Federal Infrastructure Investment Advancing Equity Goals?* Washington, DC: Urban Institute, October 2023.

Fry, Chris. "New Report Details the Depths of Jersey City's Housing Shortage." *Jersey Digs*, December 17, 2024.

Galper, Harvey, Kim Rueben, Richard Auxier C, and Amanda Eng. *Municipal Debt: What Does It Buy and Who Benefits?* Urban Institute, 2014. https://www.urban.org/sites/default/files/publication/33631/109047-municipal-debt-what-does-it-buy-and-who-benefits-.pdf.

Galper, Harvey, Kim Rueben, Richard Auxier, and Amanda Eng. *Municipal Debt: What Does It Buy and Who Benefits?* Washington, DC: Urban Institute, December 2014.

Glynn, Kendall. "White Atlanta Families Have 46 Times More Wealth than Black Ones. How Do We Fix That?" *Atlanta Civic Circle*, January 17, 2024. https://atlantaciviccircle.org/2024/01/17/atlanta-racial-wealth-gap-solutions/.

Greenberg, David M., et al. "Housing Speculation, Affordable Investments, and Tenant Outcomes in New York City." *Cityscape* 26, no. 1 (2024): 153–177.

Harvard Joint Center for Housing Studies. "Discrimination in Home Lending and Appraisals: Challenges for Black Homebuyers in Massachusetts." JCHS□Housing□Blog. Accessed February 22, 2026. https://www.jchs.harvard.edu/blog/discrimination-home-lending-and-appraisals-challenges-black-homebuyers-massachusetts.

Harvey, David. "The Neoliberal State." In *A Brief History of Neoliberalism*. Oxford: Oxford University Press, 2005.

Herbert, Christopher, E, Donald Haurin H, Stuart Rosenthal S, and Mark Duda. "Homeownership Gaps Among Low-Income and Minority Borrowers and Neighborhoods." In

HUD User. Department of Housing and Urban Development, Office of Policy Development and Research, 2005. https://www.huduser.gov/publications/pdf/homeownership gapsamonglow-incomeandminority.pdf.

Hernandez, Alex, V. "Neighbors Overwhelmingly Reject Expanding Pilsen TIF, Survey Shows." *Block Club Chicago*, August 15, 2025. https://blockclubchicago.org/2025/08/15/neighbors-overwhelmingly-reject-expanding-pilsen-tif-survey-shows/.

Hoagland, Stephanie M. "Preservation Stagnation on the Jersey Shore." *National Park Service*. Accessed February 21, 2026. https://www.nps.gov/articles/000/preservation-stagnation-on-the-jersey-shore.htm

Hornung, Daniel. *States Can Ensure New Low-Income Housing Resources Get More Affordable Housing Built*. Washington, DC: Urban Institute, July 2025.

Horsley, Lynn. "Despite Large Power & Light District Crowds, Taxpayers Are Still on the Hook." *Kansas City Star*, February 7, 2015. https://www.kansascity.com/news/politics-government/article9530081.html#storylink=cpy.

Ihnen, Alex. "St. Louis Outlet Mall Sells for 98% Off." NextSTL, February 25, 2016. https://nextstl.com/2016/02/st-louis-outlet-mall-sells-98-off/.

Illinois Policy Institute. "Mayor Johnson's Record-Setting $1 Billion TIF Surplus Highlights Issues and Abuse of Chicago's Tax Increment Financing Districts." Illinois Policy Institute, December 3, 2025.

https://www.illinoispolicy.org/mayor-johnsons-record-setting-1-billion-tif-surplus-highlights-issues-and-abuse-of-chicagos-tax-increment-financing-districts/.

Illinois Policy Institute. "Report: Chicago Lost Out on 43,000 Homes Because of Zoning Mandates." Press release, October 1, 2025.

Independent Budget Office. *Exemption or Abatement? Structure of Proposed New 421-a Program Has Implications for All Property Tax Bills.* Independent Budget Office, 2024. https://www.ibo.nyc.ny.us/iboreports/exemption-or-abatement-structure-of-proposed-new-412-a-program-has-implications-for-all-property-tax-bills-march-2024.pdf.

Jackson, Dylan. "Atlanta Has the Highest Income Inequality in the Nation, Census Data Shows." *Atlanta Journal-Constitution*, November 28, 2022. https://www.ajc.com/news/investigations/atlanta-has-the-highest-income-inequality-in-the-nation-census-data-shows/YJRZ6A4UGBFWTMYICTG2BCOUPU/.

Jaffe, Maxwell, and Dustin Ingram. "Expirations and Early Exits of LIHTC Units." *Chicago Fed Letter*, no. 514 (October 16, 2025).

Joseph, Mark L. "Is Mixed-Income Development an Antidote to Urban Poverty?" *Housing Policy Debate* 17, no. 2 (2006): 209–234.

Khare, Amy T. "Market-Driven Public Housing Reforms." *Cityscape* 15, no. 2 (2013): 193–204.

Klein, Aaron, and Alan Cui. "Quantitative Easing and Housing Inflation Post-COVID." Brookings Institution, October 8, 2025.

Lens, Michael C. "Zoning, Land Use, and the Reproduction of Urban Inequality." *Annual Review of Sociology* 48 (2022): 421–439.

Lim, Sungwoo, et al. "Impact of Residential Displacement on Healthcare Access and Mental Health." *PLoS ONE* 12, no. 12 (2017): e0190139.

Logan, John, R, and Harvey Molotch L. *Urban Fortunes: The Political Economy of Place, 20th Anniversary Edition.* 2007; University of California Press, n.d.

Louie, Schuyler, John Mondragon, Rami Najjar, and Johannes F. Wieland. "Housing Affordability and Housing Demand." *FRBSF Economic Letter* 2026-03 (February 2, 2026).

Lui, Meizhu, Bárbara J. Robles, Betsy Leondar-Wright, Rose Brewer M, and Rebecca Adamson. *The Color of Wealth: The Story Behind the U.S. Racial Wealth Divide* . The New Press, 2006. https://doi.org/10.2307/jj.25291679.

Lui, Meizhu, et al. *The Color of Wealth*. New York: The New Press, 2006.

Maryland Department of Housing and Community Development. "ReBUILD Metro." Press release, July 30, 2025.

Melamed, Jodi. "Racial Capitalism." *Critical Ethnic Studies* 1, no. 1 (2015): 76–85.

Merriam-Webster. "Definition of Gentry."
Merriam-Webster. Accessed February 21, 2026.
https://www.merriam-webster.com/dictionary/gentry.

Metro Atlanta Chamber, . "Downtown Atlanta: A Center of
Growth, Investment, and Opportunity." Metro Atlanta
Chamber, January.
https://metroatlantachamber.com/downtown-atlanta-a-
center-of-growth-investment-and-opportunity/.

Michel, Norbert J. *Strict Bank-Like Capital Rules Needed
for Fannie Mae and Freddie Mac*. Heritage Foundation,
2020.

Michener, Jamila, ed. *Poverty & Race* 32, no. 1 (2023).

Molotch, Harvey. "The city as a Growth Machine: Toward
a Political Economy of Place." *American Journal of
Sociology* 82, no. 2 (1976): 309 - 332.
https://doi.org/10.2307/2777096.

Moody's Investors Service. *Moody's Rating Symbols and
Definitions*. Moody's Investors Service, n.d. Accessed
February 22, 2026.
https://www.moodys.com/sites/products/productattachment
s/ap075378_1_1408_ki.pdf.

Morrissey, Timothy W., et al. "Household Economic
Instability." *Child & Youth Services Review* 118 (2020):
105502.

Moy, Jeffrey. "Downtown vs. the Mall: The Story of
Morristown's Headquarters Plaza, and Urban Renewal in
Morris County." Morristown Green, November 2, 2019.
https://morristowngreen.com/2019/11/02/downtown-vs-

the-mall-the-story-of-morristowns-headquarters-plaza-and-urban-renewal-in-morris-county/.

National Community Reinvestment Coalition (NCRC). "Opportunity Zones: A Taxpayer-Funded Program That Primarily Benefits Wealthy Investors." National Community Reinvestment Coalition (NCRC), October 8, 2025. https://ncrc.org/opportunity-zones-a-taxpayer-funded-program-that-primarily-benefits-wealthy-investors/.

National Community Reinvestment Coalition. "Gentrification and Disinvestment 2020□» NCRC." In *National Community Reinvestment Coalition*. Washington, DC, 2020. https://ncrc.org/gentrification20.

Neavling, Steve. "Black Detroiters Are Fleeing the City at an Alarming Rate." *Metro Times*, March 29–April 4, 2023.

Ortiz-Grabe, Luke. *A Look Over the Mountain: The Triumph of Denver's Five Points Neighborhood.* Senior Division Historical Paper, n.d. https://clas.ucdenver.edu/nhdc/sites/default/files/attached-files/entry_433.pdf.

Perry, Andre M., and Hannah Stephens. "Investment without Displacement." Brookings Institution, January 24, 2024.

Peter, Tobias. "Philadelphia's Property Tax Abatement Success Story." *City Journal* accessed February 3, 2026.

Pittsburgh Community Reinvestment Group. *Black Homeownership Report: Taking Stock – A Decade in Decline for Black Homeownership in Pittsburgh.* Pittsburgh Community Reinvestment Group, 2022. https://www.pcrg.org/black-homeownership-report.

Preziuso, Danielle, and Philip Odonkor. "Governance Gaps in Urban Decarbonization." *Energy & Environmental Sustainability* 1, no. 4 (2025): 100054.

Prytherch, David L. "Reimagining the Physical/Social Infrastructure." *Urban Geography* 43, no. 5 (2022): 688–712.

Pujols, Chelsea. "As Rents Surge in Jersey City, Mayoral Candidates Offer Diverging Plans on Affordable Housing • The Jersey Vindicator." The Jersey Vindicator, July 22, 2025. https://jerseyvindicator.org/2025/07/22/as-rents-surge-in-jersey-city-mayoral-candidates-offer-diverging-plans-on-affordable-housing/.

Resident Staff. "JLL Secures $384 Million for Jersey City's Harborside 8 Luxury Waterfront Development." *Resident Magazine*, December 26, 2025. https://resident.com/press-releases/2025/12/26/jll-secures-384-million-for-jersey-citys-harborside-8-luxury-waterfront-development.

Robinson, Cedric, J. "Oliver Cromwell Cox and the Historiography of the West." In *On Racial Capitalism, Black Internationalism, and Cultures of Resistance*. Pluto Press, 2019.

Robinson, Cedric, J. *Black Marxism: The Making of the Black Radical Tradition*. Pluto Press, 2019.

Rosenblum, Constance. "A Wildwood Makeover." *New York Times*, July 1, 2005. https://www.nytimes.com/2005/07/01/realestate/a-wildwood-makeover.html

Rothstein, Richard. *The Color of Law: A Forgotten History of How Our Government Segregated America*. Liveright Publishing, 2017.

Roy, Ananya, Wendy Larner, and Jamie Peck. "Book Review Symposium." *Progress in Human Geography* 36, no. 2 (2012): 273–281.

Saito, Leland. "How Low-Income Residents Can Benefit from Urban Development: The L.A. Live Community Benefits Agreement." *City & Community* 11, no. 2 (2012): 119 - 150. https://journals.sagepub.com/doi/10.1111/j.1540-6040.2012.01399.x.

Schilling, Joseph, Samantha Fu, and Yonah Freemark. *Promoting Equitable Development in Communities*. Washington, DC: Urban Institute, June 2024.

Schlossberg, Dina. "What Do We Talk About When We Talk About Gentrification?" *Journal of Affordable Housing & Community Development Law* 25, no. 2 (2017): 215 - 218. https://doi.org/10.2307/26408186.

Schneider, Benjamin. "Learning from Jersey City." Vital City, September 17, 2025. https://www.vitalcitynyc.org/articles/learning-from-jersey-city.

Schneider, Jakob Kendall, Mary Clare Lennon, and Susan Saegert. "Do Community Land Trusts Improve Resident Outcomes?" Housing Matters, Urban Institute, February 21, 2024.

Setterfield, Mark. Review of *Austerity*, by Mark Blyth. *Eastern Economic Journal* 44 (2018): 335–336.

Smith, Molly, and Danielle Moran. "Up Against Wall Street Bond Giants, Minority Firms Want More." *Bloomberg*, December 17, 2020. https://www.bloomberg.com/news/articles/2020-12-17/up-against-wall-street-bond-giants-minority-firms-want-more.

Smith, Talmon Joseph. "A Municipal Debt Boom Is Driving Public Projects." *New York Times*, January 28, 2026.

Smothers, Ronald. "In New Jersey, Morristown Renewal Still Debated." *The New York Times*, June 23, 1985. https://www.nytimes.com/1985/06/23/realestate/in-new-jersey-morristown-renewal-still-debated.html.

State of New Jersey Department of Community Affairs. *Annual Action Plan 2023*. Trenton, NJ, 2023.

Taylor, Keeanga-Yamahtta. "Let the Buyer Beware." In *Race for Profit: How Banks and the Real Estate Industry Undermined Black Homeownership*. North Carolina Scholarship Online, 2021.

Taylor, Keeanga-Yamahtta. *Race for Profit: How Banks and the Real Estate Industry Undermined Black Homeownership*. University of North Carolina Press, 2019.

Taylor, Sri, and Amanda Albright. "CIM-Backed Revamp of Atlanta Downtown to Tap Muni Market." *Bloomberg*, August 15, 2024. https://www.bloomberg.com/news/articles/2024-08-15/cim-backed-revamp-of-atlanta-downtown-to-tap-muni-market.

Theodos, Brett, Eric Hangen, Brady Meixell, and Lionel Foster. *The East Baltimore Development Initiative: A Long-Term Impact Evaluation of a Comprehensive Community Initiative.* Urban Institute, 2022.

Theodos, Brett, Eric Hangen, Jorge González, and Brady Meixell. *An Early Assessment of Opportunity Zones for Equitable Development Projects.* Urban Institute, 2018. https://www.urban.org/sites/default/files/publication/10234 8/early-assessment-of-opportunity-zones-for-equitable-development-projects.pdf.

Theodos, Brett, et al. *The East Baltimore Development Initiative.* Washington, DC: Urban Institute, November 2022.

U.S. Census Bureau. "Median Monthly Housing Costs (Dollars)." American Community Survey, ACS 5-Year Estimates Detailed Tables, Table B25105, 2026. https://data.census.gov/table/ACSDT5Y2024.B25105?g=0 40XX00US34,34_050XX00US34017,34017_060XX00US 3401736000,3401736000_1400000US34017004600. Accessed on 19 Feb 2026.

U.S. Census Bureau. "U.S. Census Bureau QuickFacts: Morristown Town, New Jersey." U.S. Census Bureau. Accessed February 21, 2026. https://www.census.gov/quickfacts/fact/table/morristownto wnnewjersey/PST045225#PST045225.

U.S. Department of Housing and Urban Development. "Opportunity Zones." Dataset, HUD User GIS Open Data. Accessed February 21, 2026. https://hudgis-hud.opendata.arcgis.com/datasets/HUD::opportunity-zones/explore?location=28.420892%2C0.315564%2C0.

U.S. Department of Housing and Urban Development. "Opportunity Zones." ArcGIS Open Data. Accessed February 22, 2026. https://hudgis-hud.opendata.arcgis.com/datasets/HUD::opportunity-zones/explore.

U.S. Department of Housing and Urban Development. *Opportunity Zones Dataset*. HUD GIS Open Data, 2026. https://hudgis-hud.opendata.arcgis.com/datasets/HUD::opportunity-zones/explore?location=28.420892%2C0.315564%2C0.

U.S. Department of Housing and Urban Development. *U.S. Department of Housing and Urban Development*. Dataset, HUDGIS Open Data. n.d. Accessed February 22, 2026. https://hudgis-hud.opendata.arcgis.com/datasets/HUD::opportunity-zones/explore?location=40.691192%2C-73.996966%2C14.

Ulloa, Daniel. "Jersey City Council Votes in Favor of 30-Year PILOT for Paulus Hook Development." Hudson County View, October 9, 2025. https://hudsoncountyview.com/jersey-city-council-votes-in-favor-of-30-year-pilot-for-paulus-hook-development/.

United States Census Bureau QuickFacts. "U.S. Census Bureau QuickFacts: Hoboken City, New Jersey." Accessed February 21, 2026. https://www.census.gov/quickfacts/fact/table/hobokencitynewjersey/PST045224.

United States Census Bureau. "Median Value (Dollars)." American Community Survey, ACS 1-Year Estimates Detailed Tables, Table B25077, 2026. https://data.census.gov/table/ACSDT1Y2024.B25077?g=0

40XX00US34,34_050XX00US34017,34017_060XX00US
3401736000,3401736000_1400000US34017004600.

University of Richmond Digital Scholarship Lab. *Mapping
Inequality: Redlining in New Deal America*. Denver,
Colorado, Area Description D13. University of Richmond
Digital Scholarship Lab, n.d. Accessed February 22, 2026.
https://dsl.richmond.edu/panorama/redlining/map/CO/Denv
er/area_descriptions/D13.

University of Richmond Digital Scholarship Lab. *Mapping
Inequality: Redlining in New Deal America, Redlining Map
and Area Descriptions for Denver, CO*. University of
Richmond Digital Scholarship Lab, n.d. Accessed February
22, 2026.
https://dsl.richmond.edu/panorama/redlining/map/CO/Denv
er/area_descriptions#mapview=full&loc=14/39.763/-
104.9511.

University of Richmond Digital Scholarship Lab. *Mapping
Inequality: Redlining in New Deal America, Redlining Map
and Area Descriptions for Manhattan, NY (Including
Harlem)*. University of Richmond Digital Scholarship Lab,
2026.
https://dsl.richmond.edu/panorama/redlining/map/NY/Man
hattan/area_descriptions#mapview=full&loc=12/40.7897/-
73.9625.

University of Richmond Digital Scholarship Lab. *Mapping
Inequality: Redlining in New Deal America, Redlining Map
for Brooklyn, NY (Including DUMBO, Williamsburg,
Bushwick)*. University of Richmond Digital Scholarship
Lab, n.d. Accessed February 22, 2026.
https://dsl.richmond.edu/panorama/redlining/map.

University of Richmond Digital Scholarship Lab. *Mapping Inequality: Redlining in New Deal America, Redlining Map for Brooklyn, NY (Including DUMBO, Williamsburg, Bushwick)*. University of Richmond Digital Scholarship Lab, n.d. Accessed February 22, 2026. https://dsl.richmond.edu/panorama/redlining/map/NY/Brooklyn/areas#mapview=full&loc=12/40.6551/-73.9488.

Urban Displacement Project. "Los Angeles – Gentrification and Displacement." Accessed January 31, 2026.

Vesecky, Daniel. "Understanding Chicago's 2026 Record TIF Surplus." Civic Federation, December 1, 2025. https://www.civicfed.org/understanding-chicagos-2026-record-tif-surplus.

Weber, Rachel. "Embedding Futurity in Urban Governance." *Environment and Planning A* 53, no. 3 (2021): 503–524.

———. "Fast Money Builds the Speculative City." In *From Boom to Bubble*. Chicago: University of Chicago Press, 2015.

Wetzstein, Steffen. "The Global Urban Housing Affordability Crisis." *Urban Studies* 54, no. 14 (2017): 3159 - 3177. https://doi.org/10.2307/26428376.

Wetzstein, Steffen. "The Global Urban Housing Affordability Crisis." *Urban Studies* 54, no. 14 (2017): 3159–3177.

Wileden, Lydia. *Evaluating Variation in Neighborhood Sentiments Among Strategic Neighborhood Fund Residents*. Detroit Metro Area Communities Study, June 2024.

Woldoff, Rachael A. Review of *Stuck in Place*, by Patrick Sharkey. *American Journal of Sociology* 121, no. 1 (2015): 288–290.

Wolfson, Charlie. "2020 Census: Pittsburgh's Slight Decline Came with 'Massive' Demographic Shifts in 2010s." *Public Source*, August 13, 2021. https://www.publicsource.org/pittsburgh-allegheny-county-census-2020/.

Woods, Christopher. *Allentown's Neighborhood Improvement Zone: Five Years of Failed Community and Economic Development.* Lehigh Preserve Institutional Repository, 2019.

Zandi, Mark, and Cristian deRitis. *The Case for Lower FHA Premiums.* Moody's Analytics, 2015. https://www.economy.com/getlocal?q=5cc421dd-4480-4961-b576-2594d0aab92e&app=eccafile.

Zhang, Cong, et al. "The Role of ESG Performance." *Research in International Business and Finance* 70 (2024): 102358.

Zuk, Miriam, et al. "Gentrification, Displacement, and the Role of Public Investment." *Journal of Planning Literature* 33, no. 1 (2017): 31–44.

9 798995 165811